D0315799

Addition and Subtraction Applied to Clocks

An Arithmetic Workbook to Practice Adding and Subtracting Hours and Minutes to and from Time

Chris McMullen, Ph.D.

Addition and Subtraction Applied to Clocks: An Arithmetic Workbook to Practice Adding and Subtracting Hours and Minutes to and from Time

Copyright (c) 2010 Chris McMullen, Ph.D.

All rights reserved. This includes the right to reproduce any portion of this book in any form. However, teachers who purchase one copy of this book, or borrow one physical copy from a library, may make and distribute photocopies of selected pages for instructional purposes for their own classes only. Also, parents who purchase one copy of this book, or borrow one physical copy from a library, may make and distribute photocopies of selected pages for use by their own children only.

CreateSpace

Nonfiction / Education / Elementary School / Arithmetic
Children's / Science / Mathematics / Arithmetic
Professional & Technical / Education / Specific Skills / Mathematics

ISBN: 145363228X

EAN-13: 9781453632284

Contents

Introduction

This workbook is designed to challenge students to apply their basic arithmetic skills to the concept of time. These exercises require some thought in addition to arithmetic. For example, suppose that it's presently 11:45 a.m. and you have an appointment at 1:30 p.m. How much time you have before your appointment is an important measure to be able to work out. The problem is not as trivial as subtracting 11:45 a.m. from 1:30 p.m. That is, a student who tries to set up a subtraction problem of the form, 130 – 1145 will (should!) immediately see that this won't work. Even if you want to perform the simpler subtraction problem, 3:30 p.m. from 5:45 p.m., a subtraction of the form, 545 – 330 does not provide the correct answer. The reason, of course, is that there are 60 minutes, rather than 100 minutes, in each hour. There are two additional complications to applying arithmetic to modern clocks: (1) Time is cyclic – that is, after the 12 o'clock hour, next comes the 1 o'clock hour, and (2) the 24-hour period is divided into two 12-hour durations. In order to solve these problems, students will have to think their way through the hours and minutes of the day.

These problems teach some important skills. For one, students will get additional practice building their arithmetic fluency. Also, students will get early experience applying learned concepts to practical situations. Another important skill is that the thought process learned here is very fundamental toward learning how to solve word problems. These problems don't have words, but do require students to grasp and apply concepts, which are essential skills for being able to solve word problems. The challenge of applying arithmetic concepts to time can also serve as a useful way to engage advanced and gifted students who are otherwise reluctant to practice their basic arithmetic skills.

This book is conveniently divided up into five chapters. Each chapter focuses on either addition or subtraction. The first two chapters involve just adding and subtracting minutes from times. The next two chapters include both hours and minutes. The final chapter involves figuring out how many hours and minutes two given times are apart. Organized in this way, students can focus on learning one aspect of the problem at a time. The first page of each chapter provides a concise description of the problem-solving strategy followed by 4 to 5 examples. These examples should serve to guide the student's reasoning until the student is able to successfully solve the problems on a consistent basis. However, students may find another way to solve the problems; some methods may work only for some problems, while others may work for all of the problems. Creative problem-solving is a practical skill, so use of alternative methods should be encouraged so long as they consistently produce correct answers.

The answers to the exercises are tabulated in the back of the book. Students should do their best to solve the problem first and then check the answers. Students should rework any solutions for which the answers were incorrect so that they may learn from their mistakes. Teachers and parents are encouraged to motivate their students and children to express their ideas on paper – that is, to show all of their work. It is important to learn early on to write your ideas – in math and/or words – on paper when solving problems. Ask the students how they solved the problems: It's important that they actually understand what they are doing and why, not just that they can reproduce the problem-solving strategies.

Chapter 1: Practice Adding Minutes to Times

Notes: There are 60 minutes in one hour. There are 12 morning (a.m.) hours and 12 afternoon/evening (p.m.) hours in one day. The morning (a.m.) hours begin at midnight and end at noon, and the afternoon/evening (p.m.) hours begin at noon and end at midnight. So, for example, 12:01 a.m. comes 2 minutes after 11:59 p.m., while 12:01 p.m. comes 2 minutes after 11:59 a.m. As you pass noon, you go from a.m. to p.m., and as you pass midnight, you go from p.m. to a.m.

Instructions:
- In order to add minutes to a given time, first figure out the total number of minutes – the minutes of the given time and the minutes you are adding to it.
- If the total number of minutes is 60 or more, subtract 60 minutes from the total number of minutes and increase the hours by one. If the total number of minutes is still 60 or more, repeat this step until it is not.
- If the time passes noon, change a.m. to p.m. If it passes midnight, change p.m. to a.m.
- If the hours are 13 or more, subtract 12 from the hours.
- The hours and minutes together form the new time.

Example 1: Add 23 min. to 4:35 a.m.
The total number of minutes is $23 + 35 = 58$ min. This is less than 60 min., so the hours don't change. The answer is 4:58 a.m.

Example 2: Add 46 min. to 8:27 p.m.
The total number of minutes is $46 + 27 = 73$ min. This is greater than 59 min., so we subtract 60 minutes: $73 - 60 = 13$ min. Since we subtracted 60 minutes once, we must increase the hours by one: $8 + 1 = 9$ hr. The answer is 9:13 p.m.

Example 3: Add 17 min. to 11:53 a.m.
The total number of minutes is $17 + 53 = 70$ min. This is greater than 59 min., so we subtract 60 minutes: $70 - 60 = 10$ min. Since we subtracted 60 minutes once, we must increase the hours by one: $11 + 1 = 12$ hr. Since the time passes noon, we must change a.m. to p.m. The answer is 12:10 p.m.

Example 4: Add 90 min. to 11:48 p.m.
The total number of minutes is $90 + 48 = 138$ min. This is greater than 59 min., so we subtract 60 minutes: $138 - 60 = 78$ min. It is still greater than 59 min., so we do it again: $78 - 60 = 18$ min. Since we subtracted 60 minutes twice, we must increase the hours by two: $11 + 2 = 13$ hr. Since the time passes midnight, we must change p.m. to a.m. The hours exceed 12, so we subtract 12 hours: $13 - 12 = 1$ hr. The answer is 1:18 a.m.

9:35 a.m. + 1 min. =

11:57 a.m. + 92 min. =

8:36 p.m. + 4 min. =

12:13 a.m. + 47 min. =

12:58 a.m. + 24 min. =

2:18 a.m. + 43 min. =

11:27 p.m. + 11 min. =

10:39 a.m. + 81 min. =

12:04 a.m. + 100 min. =

6:11 p.m. + 38 min. =

2:55 a.m. + 10 min. =   7:50 p.m. + 27 min. =

12:04 a.m. + 1 min. =   12:54 a.m. + 83 min. =

2:51 p.m. + 32 min. =   8:13 a.m. + 37 min. =

4:21 p.m. + 48 min. =   4:21 p.m. + 77 min. =

8:00 a.m. + 98 min. =   11:25 p.m. + 34 min. =

10:13 p.m. + 47 min. =   5:52 p.m. + 79 min. =

7:07 p.m. + 79 min. =   1:08 a.m. + 46 min. =

10:24 p.m. + 81 min. =   10:05 a.m. + 58 min. =

10:50 p.m. + 65 min. =   2:00 p.m. + 82 min. =

6:45 p.m. + 99 min. =   11:50 a.m. + 79 min. =

8:26 a.m. + 42 min. =   9:31 p.m. + 48 min. =

8:49 p.m. + 6 min. =   4:20 a.m. + 40 min. =

8:23 a.m. + 84 min. =   6:05 p.m. + 37 min. =

4:26 a.m. + 9 min. =   12:17 p.m. + 47 min. =

1:02 a.m. + 31 min. =   12:09 p.m. + 99 min. =

4:33 a.m. + 47 min. =

11:55 p.m. + 26 min. =

8:42 a.m. + 49 min. =

5:08 a.m. + 84 min. =

1:22 a.m. + 72 min. =

6:53 a.m. + 27 min. =

9:39 p.m. + 53 min. =

9:50 p.m. + 38 min. =

2:03 p.m. + 29 min. =

12:07 a.m. + 5 min. =

7:36 a.m. + 40 min. =

5:31 p.m. + 36 min. =

6:15 a.m. + 94 min. =

4:30 a.m. + 26 min. =

5:01 a.m. + 92 min. =

2:41 a.m. + 79 min. =

4:24 a.m. + 39 min. =

8:39 p.m. + 93 min. =

3:08 p.m. + 8 min. =

7:43 p.m. + 65 min. =

6:51 p.m. + 32 min. =   10:22 a.m. + 56 min. =

2:32 a.m. + 98 min. =   6:05 p.m. + 71 min. =

2:53 a.m. + 7 min. =   1:41 a.m. + 24 min. =

7:12 a.m. + 18 min. =   2:48 p.m. + 63 min. =

5:12 p.m. + 87 min. =   4:47 p.m. + 34 min. =

7:30 p.m. + 86 min. =   12:55 a.m. + 20 min. =

1:24 p.m. + 32 min. =   5:56 p.m. + 75 min. =

12:39 a.m. + 11 min. =   6:28 p.m. + 30 min. =

8:58 p.m. + 54 min. =   5:16 a.m. + 1 min. =

3:38 p.m. + 90 min. =   2:21 p.m. + 25 min. =

5:52 p.m. + 88 min. =   4:33 p.m. + 45 min. =

8:53 p.m. + 76 min. =   8:25 p.m. + 78 min. =

8:42 a.m. + 70 min. =   12:53 p.m. + 22 min. =

8:14 a.m. + 94 min. =   11:25 p.m. + 96 min. =

6:09 a.m. + 59 min. =   6:14 p.m. + 24 min. =

4:42 a.m. + 76 min. =   11:17 a.m. + 66 min. =

10:17 p.m. + 86 min. =   3:20 p.m. + 39 min. =

3:31 p.m. + 7 min. =   2:19 a.m. + 6 min. =

3:10 a.m. + 21 min. =   8:49 a.m. + 4 min. =

12:34 a.m. + 72 min. =   8:13 p.m. + 46 min. =

3:32 a.m. + 28 min. =   7:05 a.m. + 32 min. =

10:39 a.m. + 67 min. =   12:08 p.m. + 47 min. =

7:04 a.m. + 79 min. =   7:32 p.m. + 90 min. =

11:15 a.m. + 83 min. =   3:12 a.m. + 2 min. =

9:33 a.m. + 38 min. =   10:16 p.m. + 70 min. =

11:50 p.m. + 74 min. =   9:37 p.m. + 93 min. =

6:00 a.m. + 98 min. =   3:58 p.m. + 20 min. =

3:35 p.m. + 77 min. =   7:25 p.m. + 26 min. =

9:09 a.m. + 86 min. =   11:14 a.m. + 19 min. =

10:22 p.m. + 8 min. =   2:57 p.m. + 19 min. =

3:46 p.m. + 39 min. =

10:59 a.m. + 12 min. =

11:45 p.m. + 89 min. =

8:59 p.m. + 55 min. =

12:03 p.m. + 86 min. =

10:58 a.m. + 31 min. =

5:08 a.m. + 15 min. =

5:11 a.m. + 98 min. =

9:24 p.m. + 90 min. =

10:31 p.m. + 74 min. =

10:16 p.m. + 64 min. =   12:05 p.m. + 17 min. =

9:03 a.m. + 29 min. =   1:03 a.m. + 21 min. =

4:30 a.m. + 16 min. =   5:21 p.m. + 13 min. =

11:47 p.m. + 73 min. =   4:45 p.m. + 93 min. =

2:38 p.m. + 98 min. =   5:18 p.m. + 68 min. =

9:13 p.m. + 87 min. =   6:46 a.m. + 75 min. =

6:10 a.m. + 91 min. =   12:49 a.m. + 96 min. =

11:28 p.m. + 53 min. =   12:29 a.m. + 75 min. =

5:27 p.m. + 73 min. =   8:26 p.m. + 48 min. =

1:16 a.m. + 10 min. =   6:43 a.m. + 93 min. =

12:41 p.m. + 5 min. =   9:12 a.m. + 16 min. =

1:44 a.m. + 35 min. =   6:20 p.m. + 5 min. =

1:36 a.m. + 92 min. =   2:01 p.m. + 54 min. =

6:06 p.m. + 4 min. =   1:18 p.m. + 43 min. =

1:51 a.m. + 39 min. =   7:37 a.m. + 37 min. =

1:18 p.m. + 90 min. =   7:46 a.m. + 28 min. =

8:16 p.m. + 38 min. =   7:43 p.m. + 59 min. =

12:58 a.m. + 41 min. =   12:25 p.m. + 60 min. =

8:53 a.m. + 37 min. =   4:08 p.m. + 47 min. =

4:43 p.m. + 24 min. =   12:57 a.m. + 27 min. =

3:26 p.m. + 33 min. =   9:01 p.m. + 25 min. =

6:30 a.m. + 80 min. =   9:14 p.m. + 57 min. =

10:13 a.m. + 22 min. =   9:42 p.m. + 92 min. =

10:23 p.m. + 96 min. =   4:54 a.m. + 99 min. =

6:50 p.m. + 46 min. =   8:38 p.m. + 69 min. =

6:34 p.m. + 21 min. =   8:22 a.m. + 59 min. =

6:44 a.m. + 100 min. =   10:40 a.m. + 64 min. =

8:48 p.m. + 31 min. =   11:46 p.m. + 90 min. =

11:36 a.m. + 90 min. =   2:44 p.m. + 59 min. =

1:14 a.m. + 7 min. =   9:20 p.m. + 86 min. =

6:04 p.m. + 60 min. =

12:12 a.m. + 35 min. =

5:05 a.m. + 2 min. =

1:21 p.m. + 76 min. =

5:11 p.m. + 81 min. =

6:33 a.m. + 16 min. =

7:08 a.m. + 95 min. =

2:36 p.m. + 9 min. =

9:24 p.m. + 77 min. =

5:30 a.m. + 67 min. =

11:13 p.m. + 61 min. =

8:18 p.m. + 71 min. =

6:00 p.m. + 11 min. =

9:25 a.m. + 29 min. =

6:54 a.m. + 78 min. =

11:23 p.m. + 87 min. =

10:59 a.m. + 90 min. =

5:52 p.m. + 76 min. =

8:13 a.m. + 74 min. =

10:50 a.m. + 36 min. =

10:59 a.m. + 32 min. =   9:27 a.m. + 73 min. =

3:53 a.m. + 18 min. =   12:21 p.m. + 70 min. =

10:38 a.m. + 74 min. =   5:03 a.m. + 21 min. =

4:17 a.m. + 89 min. =   8:41 p.m. + 5 min. =

6:21 a.m. + 23 min. =   2:51 p.m. + 33 min. =

6:12 a.m. + 61 min. =   8:36 p.m. + 26 min. =

4:53 p.m. + 51 min. =   9:40 p.m. + 15 min. =

8:17 a.m. + 69 min. =   11:38 a.m. + 96 min. =

2:16 a.m. + 49 min. =   7:30 p.m. + 61 min. =

4:29 p.m. + 62 min. =   3:42 p.m. + 80 min. =

9:58 p.m. + 79 min. =   12:30 p.m. + 19 min. =

11:06 p.m. + 33 min. =   1:28 a.m. + 9 min. =

11:20 p.m. + 62 min. =   10:14 a.m. + 12 min. =

12:09 p.m. + 17 min. =   2:12 p.m. + 67 min. =

10:55 a.m. + 91 min. =   7:51 p.m. + 17 min. =

3:21 a.m. + 30 min. =   6:48 p.m. + 42 min. =

2:34 a.m. + 1 min. =   1:56 a.m. + 70 min. =

10:32 p.m. + 3 min. =   2:39 p.m. + 98 min. =

11:11 a.m. + 39 min. =   9:52 p.m. + 53 min. =

6:24 a.m. + 90 min. =   8:43 a.m. + 56 min. =

Chapter 2: Practice Subtracting Minutes from Times

Notes: If the time does not have enough minutes to perform the subtraction, you borrow minutes from the hours. Each hour that you borrow equates to 60 minutes.

Instructions:
- In order to subtract minutes from a given time, first compare the minutes of the time to the number of minutes that you are subtracting.
- If the time has enough minutes to subtract, simply subtract the minutes and you are done.
- Otherwise, you need to borrow hours. Add 60 minutes to the time's minutes and reduce the hours by one. If the time still does not have enough minutes to do the subtraction, repeat this step until it does.
- If you get to 0 hours, add 12 more. For example, if you borrow 1 hour from 1:30 p.m., it becomes 12:30 p.m. and you receive 60 minutes in exchange for the hour.
- If the time passes noon, change p.m. to a.m. If it passes midnight, change a.m. to p.m.
- The hours and minutes together form the new time.

Example 1: Subtract 14 min. from 6:19 a.m.

19 minutes are enough to subtract 14 minutes: $19 - 14 = 5$ min. The answer is 6:05 a.m.

Example 2: Subtract 27 min. from 3:16 p.m.

16 minutes are not enough to subtract 27 minutes. We borrow 60 minutes, increasing the minutes to $16 + 60 = 76$ min. and reducing the hours to $3 - 1 = 2$ hr. Now we subtract the minutes: $76 - 27 = 49$ min. The answer is 2:49 p.m.

Example 3: Subtract 78 min. from 10:05 p.m.

5 minutes are not enough to subtract 78 minutes. We borrow 60 minutes, increasing the minutes to $5 + 60 = 65$ min. and reducing the hours to $10 - 1 = 9$ hr. However, 65 minutes are still not enough to subtract 78 minutes, so we do this again: $65 + 60 = 125$ min. and $9 - 1 = 8$ hr. Now we subtract the minutes: $125 - 78 = 47$ min. The answer is 8:47 p.m.

Example 4: Subtract 40 min. from 12:22 p.m.

22 minutes are not enough to subtract 40 minutes. We borrow 60 minutes, increasing the minutes to $22 + 60 = 82$ min. and reducing the hours to $12 - 1 = 11$ hr. Now we subtract the minutes: $82 - 40 = 42$ min. We passed noon, so p.m. changes to a.m. The answer is 11:42 a.m.

Example 5: Subtract 36 min. from 1:00 a.m.

There are zero minutes in 1:00 a.m. We borrow 60 minutes, increasing the minutes to $0 + 60 = 60$ min. and reducing the hours to $1 - 1 = 0$ hr. We reached zero hours, so we add 12: $0 + 12 = 12$ hr. Now we subtract the minutes: $60 - 36 = 24$ min. The answer is 12:24 a.m. (Notice that we didn't pass midnight, so it's still a.m.)

4:57 a.m. – 64 min. =   1:58 p.m. – 90 min. =

7:43 a.m. – 57 min. =   3:20 a.m. – 94 min. =

6:58 a.m. – 78 min. =   3:06 p.m. – 98 min. =

11:56 p.m. – 78 min. =   8:26 a.m. – 30 min. =

10:02 a.m. – 65 min. =   10:29 p.m. – 23 min. =

12:23 a.m. – 65 min. =   12:20 a.m. – 42 min. =

3:38 a.m. – 26 min. =   3:00 a.m. – 23 min. =

1:32 p.m. – 89 min. =   4:06 a.m. – 78 min. =

4:58 p.m. – 72 min. =   3:05 p.m. – 73 min. =

10:35 a.m. – 58 min. =   7:00 a.m. – 70 min. =

5:03 p.m. – 21 min. =   4:41 p.m. – 62 min. =

4:30 a.m. – 43 min. =   10:14 p.m. – 5 min. =

7:32 a.m. – 38 min. =   9:27 p.m. – 4 min. =

8:20 a.m. – 32 min. =   8:20 a.m. – 92 min. =

4:13 p.m. – 55 min. =   2:09 a.m. – 88 min. =

5:39 a.m. – 21 min. =   5:21 p.m. – 64 min. =

1:28 p.m. – 59 min. =   6:31 a.m. – 5 min. =

3:34 a.m. – 79 min. =   1:35 a.m. – 76 min. =

1:47 a.m. – 11 min. =   2:03 a.m. – 13 min. =

2:10 p.m. – 10 min. =   5:07 p.m. – 50 min. =

3:57 p.m. – 39 min. =   3:44 a.m. – 10 min. =

4:49 p.m. – 1 min. =   12:03 a.m. – 85 min. =

2:54 a.m. – 1 min. =   4:59 p.m. – 18 min. =

12:41 a.m. – 9 min. =   9:16 p.m. – 44 min. =

8:36 a.m. – 76 min. =   12:33 p.m. – 9 min. =

1:53 p.m. – 58 min. =   10:11 p.m. – 73 min. =

1:05 a.m. – 11 min. =   4:18 p.m. – 16 min. =

7:15 a.m. – 38 min. =   10:02 a.m. – 84 min. =

3:20 a.m. – 21 min. =   6:02 p.m. – 2 min. =

11:30 p.m. – 34 min. =   4:38 a.m. – 78 min. =

5:18 a.m. – 82 min. =   7:36 p.m. – 15 min. =

11:28 a.m. – 37 min. =   4:07 p.m. – 66 min. =

10:39 a.m. – 91 min. =   1:01 a.m. – 69 min. =

10:14 p.m. – 93 min. =   7:42 p.m. – 41 min. =

3:02 a.m. – 28 min. =   3:58 a.m. – 4 min. =

2:31 p.m. – 76 min. =   2:57 p.m. – 40 min. =

12:37 a.m. – 21 min. =   9:37 p.m. – 60 min. =

2:03 p.m. – 80 min. =   7:43 p.m. – 10 min. =

4:53 p.m. – 36 min. =   5:09 a.m. – 22 min. =

4:53 p.m. – 77 min. =   3:26 p.m. – 98 min. =

7:24 p.m. – 80 min. =   5:21 a.m. – 34 min. =

9:23 p.m. – 86 min. =   10:00 p.m. – 92 min. =

4:52 a.m. – 48 min. =   7:55 a.m. – 99 min. =

6:34 p.m. – 66 min. =   4:44 p.m. – 1 min. =

10:42 a.m. – 39 min. =   5:13 a.m. – 13 min. =

7:27 a.m. – 71 min. =

8:42 p.m. – 45 min. =

6:15 a.m. – 11 min. =

8:27 p.m. – 1 min. =

1:59 a.m. – 40 min. =

10:53 p.m. – 23 min. =

4:59 p.m. – 59 min. =

8:22 a.m. – 10 min. =

9:12 p.m. – 26 min. =

9:20 a.m. – 67 min. =

9:11 a.m. − 59 min. =   6:08 a.m. − 47 min. =

11:58 a.m. − 23 min. =   5:27 a.m. − 64 min. =

11:35 a.m. − 31 min. =   12:46 p.m. − 85 min. =

6:46 a.m. − 74 min. =   6:24 p.m. − 48 min. =

11:04 p.m. − 15 min. =   7:32 p.m. − 53 min. =

11:30 a.m. – 34 min. =   3:10 a.m. – 84 min. =

10:37 a.m. – 7 min. =   5:24 a.m. – 92 min. =

11:14 a.m. – 49 min. =   9:52 p.m. – 79 min. =

5:09 p.m. – 88 min. =   9:46 p.m. – 76 min. =

11:19 a.m. – 90 min. =   4:32 p.m. – 2 min. =

1:01 p.m. – 17 min. =   12:55 a.m. – 38 min. =

6:11 p.m. – 26 min. =   7:13 p.m. – 72 min. =

8:08 p.m. – 74 min. =   5:19 p.m. – 51 min. =

1:42 p.m. – 19 min. =   6:25 a.m. – 5 min. =

11:19 p.m. – 55 min. =   7:47 a.m. – 57 min. =

2:12 a.m. – 98 min. =   11:01 p.m. – 42 min. =

5:04 a.m. – 46 min. =   11:54 p.m. – 48 min. =

11:54 p.m. – 3 min. =   2:51 a.m. – 92 min. =

7:33 a.m. – 35 min. =   4:44 p.m. – 53 min. =

7:10 p.m. – 60 min. =   1:23 p.m. – 5 min. =

12:08 a.m. – 35 min. =   2:41 p.m. – 2 min. =

10:41 p.m. – 42 min. =   2:04 p.m. – 53 min. =

4:46 p.m. – 37 min. =   7:08 a.m. – 34 min. =

7:35 p.m. – 50 min. =   3:25 p.m. – 14 min. =

8:15 p.m. – 43 min. =   9:02 a.m. – 67 min. =

2:24 p.m. – 70 min. =   3:30 a.m. – 5 min. =

4:16 a.m. – 14 min. =   5:04 a.m. – 37 min. =

6:10 p.m. – 35 min. =   1:23 p.m. – 42 min. =

1:07 a.m. – 56 min. =   2:54 p.m. – 81 min. =

8:49 p.m. – 43 min. =   9:41 p.m. – 17 min. =

3:06 a.m. – 26 min. =   6:50 p.m. – 88 min. =

6:51 p.m. – 74 min. =   8:25 p.m. – 15 min. =

7:45 p.m. – 56 min. =   2:42 a.m. – 66 min. =

5:08 a.m. – 31 min. =   12:27 a.m. – 78 min. =

8:20 a.m. – 80 min. =   2:35 p.m. – 97 min. =

11:15 p.m. – 31 min. =   9:49 a.m. – 52 min. =

7:15 p.m. – 47 min. =   11:30 a.m. – 31 min. =

6:57 a.m. – 96 min. =   11:37 a.m. – 52 min. =

1:55 a.m. – 80 min. =   5:27 a.m. – 2 min. =

3:12 p.m. – 29 min. =   8:22 p.m. – 39 min. =

2:13 a.m. – 20 min. =   12:38 a.m. – 7 min. =

6:46 p.m. – 21 min. =   7:12 a.m. – 69 min. =

9:52 p.m. – 98 min. =   12:43 a.m. – 41 min. =

2:29 a.m. – 34 min. =   9:03 a.m. – 35 min. =

2:47 p.m. – 94 min. =   11:20 a.m. – 10 min. =

3:00 a.m. – 81 min. =   9:25 a.m. – 33 min. =

3:26 p.m. – 51 min. =   11:51 a.m. – 100 min. =

4:44 a.m. – 63 min. =   3:33 p.m. – 56 min. =

1:18 p.m. – 100 min. =   4:47 a.m. – 32 min. =

12:32 p.m. – 35 min. =   12:07 a.m. – 23 min. =

9:03 p.m. – 55 min. =   9:26 a.m. – 67 min. =

7:22 p.m. – 60 min. =   3:53 p.m. – 27 min. =

5:40 a.m. – 96 min. =   9:28 p.m. – 91 min. =

3:20 p.m. – 62 min. =   8:35 a.m. – 12 min. =

12:27 p.m. – 32 min. =   1:12 a.m. – 69 min. =

4:57 a.m. – 33 min. =   2:52 a.m. – 95 min. =

7:25 a.m. – 5 min. =   9:46 a.m. – 100 min. =

3:32 a.m. – 68 min. =   5:23 p.m. – 10 min. =

12:02 a.m. – 59 min. =   3:30 p.m. – 87 min. =

4:52 a.m. – 81 min. =   9:42 a.m. – 3 min. =

10:25 a.m. − 28 min. =   6:07 p.m. − 40 min. =

10:07 a.m. − 57 min. =   10:18 p.m. − 23 min. =

1:11 p.m. − 74 min. =   8:29 p.m. − 91 min. =

3:33 a.m. − 48 min. =   6:01 a.m. − 1 min. =

9:43 p.m. − 33 min. =   9:04 a.m. − 13 min. =

9:23 a.m. – 14 min. =   10:10 a.m. – 97 min. =

11:41 a.m. – 27 min. =   9:10 p.m. – 66 min. =

5:52 a.m. – 17 min. =   12:18 a.m. – 22 min. =

8:40 a.m. – 98 min. =   6:50 a.m. – 4 min. =

3:27 a.m. – 4 min. =   10:22 a.m. – 84 min. =

4:31 a.m. – 76 min. =   4:59 a.m. – 36 min. =

2:24 a.m. – 98 min. =   9:23 p.m. – 35 min. =

12:39 a.m. – 92 min. =   10:30 p.m. – 33 min. =

3:48 a.m. – 52 min. =   5:46 p.m. – 62 min. =

1:43 p.m. – 42 min. =   12:40 p.m. – 71 min. =

Chapter 3: Practice Adding Hours and Minutes to Times

Notes: Adding exactly 24 hours to a time has no effect on the time. For example, adding 32 hours to 1:14 p.m. is no different from adding 8 hours to 1:14 p.m. (Well, it does change the day and the date, but it does not change the time.)

Instructions:
- First add the minutes following the strategy from Chapter 1. Remember that you must add one hour for every 60 minutes that you subtract from excess minutes.
- Next add the hours. Recall that if the hours exceed 12, subtract 12 hours from the time. Also recall that a.m. changes to p.m. when the time passes noon and from p.m. to a.m. when it passes midnight. (Notice that this rule is opposite for addition and subtraction.)

Example 1: Add 3 hr. & 14 min. to 5:21 p.m.
The total number of minutes is $14 + 21 = 35$ min. The total number of hours is $3 + 5 = 8$ hr. The answer is 8:35 p.m.

Example 2: Add 6 hr. & 48 min. to 2:42 p.m.
The total number of minutes is $48 + 42 = 90$ min. This is greater than 59 min., so we subtract 60 minutes: $90 - 60 = 30$ min. Since we subtracted 60 minutes once, we must increase the hours by one: $2 + 1 = 3$ hr. Now we add the 6 hours: $3 + 6 = 9$ hr. The answer is 9:30 p.m.

Example 3: Add 17 hr. & 3 min. to 7:34 a.m.
The total number of minutes is $3 + 34 = 37$ min. The total number of hours is $17 + 7 = 24$ hr. The hours exceed 12, so we subtract 12 hours: $24 - 12 = 12$ hr. We passed noon, but we also passed midnight, so we leave a.m. unchanged. The answer is 12:37 a.m.

Example 4: Add 27 hr. & 44 min. to 10:51 p.m.
The total number of minutes is $44 + 51 = 95$ min. This is greater than 59 min., so we subtract 60 minutes: $95 - 60 = 35$ min. Since we subtracted 60 minutes once, we must increase the hours by one: $10 + 1 = 11$ hr. Now we add the 27 hours: $27 + 11 = 38$ hr. The hours exceed 12. First, we subtract 24 hours, which has no effect on the time: $38 - 24 = 14$ hr. The hours still exceed 12. Now we subtract 12 hours: $14 - 12 = 2$ hr. We pass midnight, noon, and midnight in the process of adding 27 hours, so we must change p.m. to a.m. The answer is 2:35 a.m.

Example 5: Add 40 hr. to 4:15 a.m.
There are no minutes to add so the minutes remain unchanged. The total number of hours is $40 + 4 = 44$ hr. The hours exceed 12. First, we subtract 24 hours, which has no effect on the time: $44 - 24 = 20$ hr. The hours still exceed 12. Now we subtract 12 hours: $20 - 12 = 8$ hr. We pass noon, midnight, and then noon in the process of adding 40 hours, so we must change a.m. to p.m. The answer is 8:15 p.m.

12:53 p.m. + 17 hr. & 32 min. =   12:18 a.m. + 5 hr. & 25 min. =

6:00 a.m. + 43 hr. & 44 min. =   6:10 a.m. + 6 hr. & 5 min. =

12:30 a.m. + 4 hr. & 36 min. =   1:17 p.m. + 1 hr. & 6 min. =

3:50 p.m. + 21 hr. & 57 min. =   3:25 p.m. + 43 hr. & 46 min. =

5:50 p.m. + 56 hr. & 50 min. =   8:04 a.m. + 7 hr. & 10 min. =

5:40 p.m. + 44 hr. & 9 min. =

11:06 p.m. + 3 hr. & 34 min. =

8:24 a.m. + 17 hr. & 9 min. =

10:35 p.m. + 46 hr. & 3 min. =

11:52 a.m. + 38 hr. & 4 min. =

12:51 a.m. + 30 hr. & 40 min. =

2:03 a.m. + 0 hr. & 41 min. =

1:16 a.m. + 43 hr. & 56 min. =

4:54 a.m. + 53 hr. & 38 min. =

4:02 a.m. + 30 hr. & 13 min. =

7:20 p.m. + 6 hr. & 17 min. =   3:08 p.m. + 3 hr. & 57 min. =

2:08 p.m. + 33 hr. & 45 min. =   2:06 a.m. + 20 hr. & 49 min. =

8:39 a.m. + 10 hr. & 34 min. =   11:58 p.m. + 43 hr. & 11 min. =

5:30 p.m. + 19 hr. & 37 min. =   4:52 p.m. + 44 hr. & 53 min. =

12:13 p.m. + 59 hr. & 25 min. =   5:17 p.m. + 36 hr. & 6 min. =

7:44 a.m. + 56 hr. & 53 min. =   11:38 p.m. + 28 hr. & 6 min. =

8:45 a.m. + 45 hr. & 16 min. =   7:56 p.m. + 49 hr. & 48 min. =

2:58 p.m. + 45 hr. & 30 min. =   1:19 a.m. + 26 hr. & 22 min. =

1:18 p.m. + 5 hr. & 20 min. =   1:33 a.m. + 3 hr. & 35 min. =

4:48 a.m. + 38 hr. & 3 min. =   11:15 a.m. + 8 hr. & 14 min. =

An Arithmetic Workbook to Practice Adding and Subtracting Hours and Minutes…

9:54 p.m. + 14 hr. & 39 min. =   10:13 p.m. + 52 hr. & 14 min. =

7:30 a.m. + 50 hr. & 13 min. =   7:03 a.m. + 26 hr. & 36 min. =

8:03 a.m. + 54 hr. & 4 min. =   11:46 a.m. + 2 hr. & 23 min. =

9:08 a.m. + 33 hr. & 56 min. =   8:30 p.m. + 51 hr. & 24 min. =

5:57 a.m. + 16 hr. & 49 min. =   2:16 p.m. + 26 hr. & 28 min. =

10:54 a.m. + 24 hr. & 35 min. =

9:01 p.m. + 34 hr. & 23 min. =

10:34 p.m. + 4 hr. & 20 min. =

11:38 p.m. + 43 hr. & 23 min. =

5:19 a.m. + 0 hr. & 30 min. =

1:28 p.m. + 12 hr. & 23 min. =

2:22 p.m. + 56 hr. & 24 min. =

5:41 p.m. + 55 hr. & 10 min. =

9:26 a.m. + 16 hr. & 1 min. =

11:30 a.m. + 23 hr. & 35 min. =

4:02 a.m. + 18 hr. & 18 min. =   6:32 a.m. + 27 hr. & 32 min. =

9:16 p.m. + 38 hr. & 53 min. =   3:38 p.m. + 42 hr. & 1 min. =

7:58 a.m. + 12 hr. & 17 min. =   11:31 p.m. + 44 hr. & 29 min. =

10:55 a.m. + 20 hr. & 40 min. =   7:03 a.m. + 36 hr. & 24 min. =

4:58 p.m. + 34 hr. & 35 min. =   9:34 a.m. + 54 hr. & 56 min. =

4:26 a.m. + 33 hr. & 3 min. =   11:04 p.m. + 54 hr. & 43 min. =

7:23 p.m. + 52 hr. & 52 min. =   10:28 a.m. + 43 hr. & 38 min. =

1:52 a.m. + 51 hr. & 49 min. =   12:27 a.m. + 40 hr. & 9 min. =

7:31 p.m. + 56 hr. & 46 min. =   11:35 a.m. + 32 hr. & 55 min. =

5:48 p.m. + 4 hr. =   12:42 a.m. + 15 hr. & 31 min. =

12:07 a.m. + 22 hr. =   2:41 p.m. + 32 hr. & 45 min. =

11:20 a.m. + 9 hr. & 36 min. =   1:09 p.m. + 25 hr. & 1 min. =

4:00 p.m. + 35 hr. & 25 min. =   1:19 p.m. + 31 hr. & 45 min. =

4:39 p.m. + 53 hr. & 54 min. =   8:11 p.m. + 53 hr. & 20 min. =

4:32 p.m. + 28 hr. & 11 min. =   10:45 p.m. + 56 hr. & 48 min. =

10:23 a.m. + 8 hr. & 47 min. =   5:41 a.m. + 38 hr. & 37 min. =

2:06 a.m. + 20 hr. & 24 min. =   6:03 a.m. + 45 hr. & 49 min. =

8:36 p.m. + 10 hr. & 2 min. =   11:39 a.m. + 14 hr. & 55 min. =

1:41 a.m. + 35 hr. & 14 min. =   3:26 a.m. + 16 hr. & 7 min. =

8:46 a.m. + 8 hr. & 27 min. =   3:29 p.m. + 24 hr. & 56 min. =

1:17 p.m. + 45 hr. & 7 min. =   4:33 a.m. + 8 hr. & 11 min. =

2:20 a.m. + 4 hr. & 34 min. =   12:40 p.m. + 59 hr. & 11 min. =

5:22 a.m. + 53 hr. & 38 min. =   6:26 a.m. + 22 hr. & 28 min. =

7:47 a.m. + 50 hr. & 52 min. =   4:05 a.m. + 48 hr. & 9 min. =

11:37 a.m. + 11 hr. & 36 min. =   8:49 a.m. + 38 hr. & 16 min. =

8:52 p.m. + 14 hr. & 4 min. =   5:06 a.m. + 4 hr. & 55 min. =

2:35 p.m. + 40 hr. & 39 min. =   10:44 a.m. + 11 hr. & 55 min. =

10:34 p.m. + 50 hr. & 12 min. =   5:47 a.m. + 54 hr. & 32 min. =

6:30 p.m. + 37 hr. & 19 min. =   2:59 a.m. + 34 hr. & 36 min. =

2:06 p.m. + 23 hr. & 34 min. =   3:14 a.m. + 27 hr. & 47 min. =

5:16 a.m. + 2 hr. & 39 min. =   3:16 a.m. + 37 hr. & 26 min. =

8:56 a.m. + 16 hr. & 17 min. =   7:48 a.m. + 45 hr. & 34 min. =

10:23 p.m. + 16 hr. & 10 min. =   3:55 a.m. + 19 hr. & 44 min. =

10:56 a.m. + 51 hr. & 59 min. =   10:13 a.m. + 32 hr. & 20 min. =

3:04 p.m. + 38 hr. & 31 min. =   11:01 a.m. + 56 hr. & 5 min. =

11:03 p.m. + 3 hr. & 15 min. =   7:59 a.m. + 22 hr. & 51 min. =

3:33 a.m. + 56 hr. & 56 min. =   4:26 p.m. + 19 hr. & 42 min. =

7:55 a.m. + 45 hr. & 40 min. =   6:54 a.m. + 23 hr. & 1 min. =

9:31 a.m. + 46 hr. & 4 min. =   8:23 a.m. + 13 hr. & 49 min. =

6:45 p.m. + 36 hr. & 16 min. =   11:39 p.m. + 11 hr. & 53 min. =

11:41 p.m. + 38 hr. & 40 min. =   2:10 a.m. + 42 hr. & 30 min. =

7:53 p.m. + 49 hr. & 10 min. =   11:06 a.m. + 37 hr. & 41 min. =

7:55 p.m. + 3 hr. & 50 min. =   12:50 a.m. + 40 hr. & 49 min. =

12:21 a.m. + 21 hr. & 34 min. =   6:56 p.m. + 49 hr. & 43 min. =

9:47 a.m. + 39 hr. & 11 min. =   9:40 p.m. + 48 hr. & 37 min. =

5:45 p.m. + 38 hr. & 52 min. =   12:52 a.m. + 29 hr. & 15 min. =

7:28 a.m. + 25 hr. & 11 min. =   4:17 p.m. + 48 hr. & 44 min. =

3:29 p.m. + 49 hr. & 44 min. =   5:20 p.m. + 29 hr. & 51 min. =

3:17 p.m. + 2 hr. & 22 min. =   1:39 p.m. + 38 hr. & 11 min. =

1:18 a.m. + 24 hr. & 56 min. =   2:20 p.m. + 17 hr. & 40 min. =

4:33 p.m. + 42 hr. & 55 min. =   10:41 a.m. + 11 hr. & 5 min. =

4:52 a.m. + 34 hr. & 44 min. =   4:53 p.m. + 51 hr. & 12 min. =

9:36 a.m. + 27 hr. & 15 min. =   11:43 p.m. + 13 hr. & 42 min. =

10:25 p.m. + 25 hr. & 49 min. =   5:59 a.m. + 44 hr. & 27 min. =

9:11 a.m. + 31 hr. & 41 min. =   2:16 p.m. + 12 hr. & 30 min. =

9:28 p.m. + 40 hr. & 15 min. =   9:55 a.m. + 41 hr. & 23 min. =

7:13 a.m. + 28 hr. & 26 min. =   10:51 a.m. + 48 hr. & 51 min. =

2:52 p.m. + 52 hr. & 33 min. =   1:11 p.m. + 27 hr. =

8:18 a.m. + 41 hr. & 46 min. =   8:56 a.m. + 45 hr. & 36 min. =

10:46 p.m. + 21 hr. & 30 min. =   8:35 p.m. + 47 hr. & 35 min. =

1:45 a.m. + 57 hr. & 38 min. =

1:01 a.m. + 45 hr. & 2 min. =

8:48 p.m. + 6 hr. & 39 min. =

4:07 p.m. + 44 hr. & 1 min. =

9:02 p.m. + 28 hr. & 45 min. =

6:48 a.m. + 10 hr. & 39 min. =

5:54 p.m. + 56 hr. & 34 min. =

9:45 a.m. + 58 hr. & 6 min. =

9:43 p.m. + 12 hr. & 9 min. =

2:28 p.m. + 30 hr. & 56 min. =

8:04 a.m. + 54 hr. & 9 min. =

5:27 a.m. + 35 hr. & 48 min. =

8:34 p.m. + 26 hr. & 13 min. =

5:29 p.m. + 10 hr. & 24 min. =

11:12 p.m. + 1 hr. & 4 min. =

10:53 a.m. + 0 hr. & 22 min. =

8:34 a.m. + 13 hr. & 15 min. =

4:28 a.m. + 24 hr. & 52 min. =

2:55 a.m. + 38 hr. & 13 min. =

1:41 a.m. + 58 hr. & 2 min. =

3:43 p.m. + 38 hr. & 34 min. =   7:07 a.m. + 35 hr. & 38 min. =

8:15 p.m. + 8 hr. & 14 min. =   3:12 p.m. + 29 hr. & 50 min. =

12:11 p.m. + 30 hr. & 38 min. =   9:27 p.m. + 34 hr. & 29 min. =

4:53 a.m. + 59 hr. & 19 min. =   1:37 a.m. + 14 hr. & 44 min. =

4:17 p.m. + 31 hr. & 30 min. =   4:26 a.m. + 59 hr. & 30 min. =

3:58 p.m. + 48 hr. & 11 min. =   6:15 p.m. + 26 hr. & 43 min. =

3:42 p.m. + 13 hr. & 58 min. =   2:31 p.m. + 15 hr. & 11 min. =

1:06 a.m. + 10 hr. & 57 min. =   1:02 a.m. + 1 hr. & 56 min. =

9:47 a.m. + 9 hr. & 9 min. =   8:35 a.m. + 23 hr. & 58 min. =

12:13 p.m. + 17 hr. & 20 min. =   11:53 a.m. + 21 hr. & 44 min. =

12:52 a.m. + 47 hr. & 36 min. =   3:48 a.m. + 48 hr. & 26 min. =

10:11 p.m. + 39 hr. & 14 min. =   7:42 a.m. + 14 hr. & 2 min. =

12:19 p.m. + 40 hr. & 10 min. =   9:13 p.m. + 25 hr. & 2 min. =

9:44 a.m. + 3 hr. & 22 min. =   10:44 a.m. + 3 hr. & 29 min. =

6:41 p.m. + 37 hr. & 54 min. =   8:35 a.m. + 58 hr. & 55 min. =

3:12 p.m. + 43 hr. & 50 min. =   11:41 a.m. + 59 hr. & 51 min. =

9:55 a.m. + 54 hr. & 24 min. =   10:07 p.m. + 52 hr. & 57 min. =

11:15 a.m. + 48 hr. & 18 min. =   2:55 p.m. + 22 hr. & 38 min. =

9:10 a.m. + 24 hr. & 32 min. =   9:40 p.m. + 43 hr. & 23 min. =

11:19 p.m. + 57 hr. & 49 min. =   8:23 a.m. + 24 hr. & 58 min. =

10:44 p.m. + 9 hr. & 36 min. =   6:31 a.m. + 53 hr. & 41 min. =

6:39 a.m. + 18 hr. & 35 min. =   3:38 p.m. + 37 hr. & 34 min. =

7:04 a.m. + 59 hr. & 50 min. =   10:55 p.m. + 12 hr. & 44 min. =

1:14 p.m. + 9 hr. & 17 min. =   2:11 a.m. + 31 hr. & 9 min. =

12:35 a.m. + 50 hr. & 13 min. =   3:49 a.m. + 16 hr. & 27 min. =

Chapter 4: Practice Subtracting Hours and Minutes from Times

Notes: Subtracting exactly 24 hours to a time has no effect on the time. For example, subtracting 40 hours from 7:54 p.m. is no different from subtracting 16 hours from 7:54 p.m. (except for changing the day and the date).

Instructions:
- First subtract the minutes following the strategy from Chapter 2. Remember that you must subtract one hour for every 60 minutes that you need to borrow.
- Next subtract the hours. If you need to borrow hours, you may add 24 hours since that has no effect on the time – or you may add 12 hours by swapping a.m. and p.m.
- Recall that p.m. changes to a.m. when the time passes noon and from a.m. to p.m. when it passes midnight.

Example 1: Subtract 8 hr. & 24 min. from 10:38 a.m.
    The total number of minutes is $38 - 24 = 14$ min. The total number of hours is $10 - 8 = 2$ hr. The answer is 2:14 a.m.

Example 2: Subtract 3 hr. & 21 min. from 1:17 p.m.
    17 minutes are not enough to subtract 21 minutes. We borrow 60 minutes, increasing the minutes to $17 + 60 = 77$ min. and reducing the hours to $1 - 1 = 0$ hr. Now we subtract the minutes: $77 - 21 = 56$ min. Since we have zero hours, we add 12 hours and change p.m. to a.m.: $0 + 12 = 12$ hr. Now we subtract hours: $12 - 3 = 9$ hr. The answer is 9:56 a.m.

Example 3: Subtract 29 hr. & 33 min. from 9:36 a.m.
    The total number of minutes is $36 - 33 = 3$ min. 9 hours are not enough to subtract 29 hours. We borrow 24 hours, increasing the hours to $9 + 24 = 33$ hr. Now we subtract the hours: $33 - 29 = 4$ hr. We passed midnight, but we also passed noon, so we leave a.m. unchanged. The answer is 4:03 a.m. (Notice that 3 minutes is written as :03.)

Example 4: Subtract 40 hr. & 18 min. from 6:15 p.m.
    15 minutes are not enough to subtract 18 minutes. We borrow 60 minutes, increasing the minutes to $15 + 60 = 75$ min. and reducing the hours to $6 - 1 = 5$ hr. Now we subtract the minutes: $75 - 18 = 57$ min. 5 hours are not enough to subtract 40 hours. We borrow 36 hours, changing p.m. to a.m. This increases the hours to $5 + 36 = 41$ hr. Now we subtract the hours: $41 - 40 = 1$ hr. The answer is 1:57 a.m.

2:25 p.m. – 14 hr. & 12 min. =   8:03 a.m. – 23 hr. & 40 min. =

4:16 p.m. – 11 hr. & 23 min. =   5:28 a.m. – 56 hr. & 27 min. =

9:44 p.m. – 21 hr. & 43 min. =   8:39 p.m. – 42 hr. & 17 min. =

4:41 a.m. – 51 hr. & 15 min. =   2:21 p.m. – 48 hr. & 56 min. =

11:33 p.m. – 15 hr. & 33 min. =   11:50 a.m. – 49 hr. & 25 min. =

4:40 p.m. – 5 hr. & 12 min. =   4:47 a.m. – 13 hr. & 17 min. =

4:04 p.m. – 12 hr. & 17 min. =   5:55 a.m. – 1 hr. & 17 min. =

2:12 a.m. – 23 hr. & 45 min. =   2:54 p.m. – 32 hr. & 9 min. =

3:35 a.m. – 26 hr. & 38 min. =   3:27 a.m. – 8 hr. & 41 min. =

9:14 p.m. – 37 hr. & 55 min. =   10:10 p.m. – 1 hr. & 54 min. =

8:18 a.m. – 3 hr. & 50 min. =

4:09 a.m. – 43 hr. & 59 min. =

11:13 p.m. – 37 hr. & 15 min. =

5:10 p.m. – 33 hr. & 26 min. =

3:29 a.m. – 14 hr. & 50 min. =

6:49 p.m. – 35 hr. =

2:24 p.m. – 10 hr. & 42 min. =

6:36 a.m. – 22 hr. & 43 min. =

5:27 p.m. – 53 hr. & 42 min. =

9:05 a.m. – 20 hr. & 50 min. =

10:15 a.m. – 48 hr. & 42 min. =   1:44 a.m. – 45 hr. & 36 min. =

9:33 a.m. – 22 hr. & 57 min. =   8:55 p.m. – 47 hr. & 18 min. =

3:12 p.m. – 7 hr. & 15 min. =   11:51 a.m. – 38 hr. & 55 min. =

11:38 p.m. – 56 hr. & 52 min. =   9:42 a.m. – 36 hr. & 25 min. =

5:59 a.m. – 3 hr. & 13 min. =   11:20 p.m. – 1 hr. & 4 min. =

1:38 a.m. – 16 hr. & 37 min. =   11:18 p.m. – 17 hr. & 2 min. =

11:33 a.m. – 14 hr. & 35 min. =   4:17 a.m. – 4 hr. & 45 min. =

8:22 a.m. – 51 hr. & 25 min. =   5:51 p.m. – 6 hr. & 44 min. =

5:04 p.m. – 11 hr. & 19 min. =   10:01 p.m. – 58 hr. & 41 min. =

3:55 a.m. – 9 hr. & 43 min. =   9:58 a.m. – 35 hr. & 59 min. =

4:15 a.m. – 21 hr. =

1:18 p.m. – 24 hr. & 19 min. =

10:16 p.m. – 57 hr. & 42 min. =

3:25 a.m. – 2 hr. & 16 min. =

4:50 p.m. – 1 hr. & 31 min. =

5:46 a.m. – 37 hr. & 21 min. =

8:36 p.m. – 45 hr. & 30 min. =

12:21 p.m. – 15 hr. & 38 min. =

12:20 a.m. – 1 hr. & 31 min. =

10:18 p.m. – 6 hr. & 7 min. =

10:28 a.m. – 10 hr. & 51 min. =   5:43 a.m. – 27 hr. & 36 min. =

7:07 p.m. – 33 hr. & 32 min. =   1:23 a.m. – 48 hr. & 12 min. =

5:19 a.m. – 5 hr. & 36 min. =   12:27 a.m. – 0 hr. & 34 min. =

12:42 p.m. – 58 hr. & 32 min. =   3:25 a.m. – 57 hr. & 51 min. =

3:49 a.m. – 35 hr. & 54 min. =   8:37 p.m. – 18 hr. & 37 min. =

7:56 p.m. – 9 hr. & 30 min. =

5:26 a.m. – 14 hr. & 22 min. =

12:28 a.m. – 35 hr. & 48 min. =

3:46 p.m. – 13 hr. & 18 min. =

9:36 a.m. – 36 hr. & 40 min. =

4:27 a.m. – 32 hr. & 43 min. =

6:15 a.m. – 22 hr. & 1 min. =

3:53 a.m. – 40 hr. & 11 min. =

10:04 p.m. – 41 hr. & 31 min. =

10:48 p.m. – 25 hr. & 15 min. =

10:32 a.m. – 42 hr. & 47 min. =   3:31 a.m. – 29 hr. & 37 min. =

9:51 p.m. – 40 hr. & 38 min. =   10:13 a.m. – 36 hr. & 11 min. =

8:16 a.m. – 42 hr. & 10 min. =   5:48 p.m. – 18 hr. & 29 min. =

10:02 a.m. – 52 hr. & 35 min. =   8:14 p.m. – 19 hr. & 18 min. =

3:49 p.m. – 16 hr. & 8 min. =   2:48 a.m. – 47 hr. & 35 min. =

7:37 a.m. – 28 hr. & 28 min. =

1:11 p.m. – 12 hr. & 51 min. =

12:26 p.m. – 20 hr. & 52 min. =

3:53 p.m. – 48 hr. & 47 min. =

1:32 p.m. – 52 hr. & 7 min. =

8:02 p.m. – 12 hr. & 17 min. =

8:53 p.m. – 29 hr. & 14 min. =

1:37 p.m. – 39 hr. & 8 min. =

5:59 p.m. – 45 hr. & 8 min. =

7:11 a.m. – 30 hr. & 31 min. =

2:17 a.m. – 17 hr. & 14 min. =   10:11 p.m. – 35 hr. & 27 min. =

7:23 a.m. – 58 hr. & 7 min. =   2:45 a.m. – 38 hr. & 13 min. =

12:04 a.m. – 42 hr. & 20 min. =   11:54 a.m. – 21 hr. & 1 min. =

10:53 a.m. – 12 hr. & 40 min. =   7:54 p.m. – 11 hr. & 51 min. =

7:36 a.m. – 52 hr. & 6 min. =   7:30 p.m. – 17 hr. & 5 min. =

5:12 p.m. – 50 hr. & 39 min. =   2:57 p.m. – 17 hr. & 32 min. =

1:19 a.m. – 45 hr. & 20 min. =   2:30 p.m. – 41 hr. & 44 min. =

12:52 p.m. – 9 hr. & 8 min. =   4:33 p.m. – 42 hr. & 7 min. =

10:05 a.m. – 12 hr. & 15 min. =   10:14 p.m. – 12 hr. & 41 min. =

3:08 a.m. – 14 hr. & 20 min. =   6:03 p.m. – 34 hr. & 47 min. =

6:00 a.m. – 53 hr. & 43 min. =   3:47 a.m. – 24 hr. & 58 min. =

8:46 p.m. – 9 hr. & 29 min. =   4:51 p.m. – 57 hr. & 34 min. =

1:10 p.m. – 34 hr. & 41 min. =   5:02 p.m. – 25 hr. & 43 min. =

10:42 p.m. – 57 hr. & 46 min. =   12:32 p.m. – 6 hr. & 56 min. =

3:17 p.m. – 43 hr. & 3 min. =   1:51 p.m. – 31 hr. & 25 min. =

8:46 a.m. – 28 hr. =   7:32 p.m. – 40 hr. & 24 min. =

1:16 p.m. – 34 hr. & 5 min. =   10:27 a.m. – 18 hr. & 23 min. =

6:05 p.m. – 1 hr. & 6 min. =   2:25 p.m. – 40 hr. & 58 min. =

1:56 a.m. – 47 hr. & 52 min. =   8:11 a.m. – 1 hr. & 47 min. =

4:48 p.m. – 21 hr. & 9 min. =   3:51 p.m. – 47 hr. & 36 min. =

10:50 p.m. – 25 hr. & 40 min. =   9:07 p.m. – 28 hr. & 39 min. =

7:38 a.m. – 13 hr. & 58 min. =   6:23 a.m. – 10 hr. & 5 min. =

10:27 a.m. – 40 hr. & 49 min. =   2:01 a.m. – 1 hr. & 19 min. =

2:27 a.m. – 50 hr. & 6 min. =   4:29 p.m. – 59 hr. & 38 min. =

6:34 a.m. – 44 hr. & 8 min. =   8:28 a.m. – 43 hr. & 37 min. =

5:45 p.m. – 11 hr. & 7 min. =   10:04 p.m. – 45 hr. & 27 min. =

2:44 a.m. – 45 hr. & 24 min. =   10:22 p.m. – 14 hr. & 24 min. =

2:28 p.m. – 43 hr. & 37 min. =   5:52 a.m. – 13 hr. & 11 min. =

2:56 a.m. – 19 hr. & 21 min. =   9:24 p.m. – 33 hr. & 55 min. =

2:05 p.m. – 26 hr. & 49 min. =   2:56 p.m. – 20 hr. & 53 min. =

2:54 a.m. – 34 hr. & 45 min. =   3:18 p.m. – 44 hr. & 25 min. =

11:30 p.m. – 28 hr. & 29 min. =   7:24 a.m. – 21 hr. & 38 min. =

8:03 p.m. – 54 hr. & 43 min. =   11:30 p.m. – 4 hr. & 54 min. =

9:18 a.m. – 24 hr. & 57 min. =   2:41 p.m. – 51 hr. & 15 min. =

4:29 p.m. – 25 hr. & 38 min. =   2:40 p.m. – 3 hr. & 16 min. =

11:22 a.m. – 28 hr. & 13 min. =   2:32 p.m. – 39 hr. & 16 min. =

7:03 a.m. – 38 hr. & 56 min. =   3:24 a.m. – 10 hr. & 52 min. =

4:20 a.m. – 36 hr. & 46 min. =   10:10 a.m. – 38 hr. & 52 min. =

9:16 p.m. – 45 hr. & 59 min. =   5:56 p.m. – 16 hr. & 56 min. =

2:18 p.m. – 32 hr. & 58 min. =   7:08 p.m. – 34 hr. & 24 min. =

7:03 a.m. – 24 hr. & 37 min. =   12:34 p.m. – 46 hr. & 38 min. =

10:07 p.m. – 12 hr. & 13 min. =   10:38 p.m. – 12 hr. & 14 min. =

10:09 p.m. – 51 hr. & 49 min. =   1:05 a.m. – 6 hr. & 43 min. =

3:58 a.m. – 17 hr. & 1 min. =   6:39 a.m. – 39 hr. =

7:37 a.m. – 42 hr. & 32 min. =   1:29 p.m. – 39 hr. & 22 min. =

10:18 a.m. – 54 hr. =   11:12 p.m. – 9 hr. & 22 min. =

4:27 a.m. – 34 hr. & 36 min. =   5:27 a.m. – 42 hr. & 36 min. =

9:43 p.m. – 59 hr. & 30 min. =   6:49 p.m. – 49 hr. & 5 min. =

3:27 p.m. – 40 hr. & 13 min. =   10:38 a.m. – 20 hr. & 56 min. =

10:51 p.m. – 15 hr. & 11 min. =   9:23 a.m. – 0 hr. & 13 min. =

2:24 a.m. – 55 hr. & 25 min. =   9:11 p.m. – 29 hr. & 59 min. =

2:44 p.m. – 43 hr. & 14 min. =   6:01 p.m. – 16 hr. & 13 min. =

5:18 p.m. – 21 hr. & 10 min. =   1:54 p.m. – 7 hr. & 16 min. =

7:29 a.m. – 19 hr. & 29 min. =   7:51 p.m. – 7 hr. & 31 min. =

11:22 p.m. – 51 hr. & 10 min. =   7:34 a.m. – 16 hr. & 16 min. =

9:04 p.m. – 1 hr. & 40 min. =

5:55 p.m. – 14 hr. & 6 min. =

11:12 a.m. – 32 hr. & 50 min. =

3:08 a.m. – 41 hr. & 36 min. =

5:07 p.m. – 6 hr. & 28 min. =

9:03 a.m. – 35 hr. =

3:47 a.m. – 16 hr. & 55 min. =

8:45 a.m. – 18 hr. & 5 min. =

2:46 a.m. – 34 hr. & 4 min. =

12:39 p.m. – 44 hr. & 52 min. =

6:36 p.m. – 3 hr. & 46 min. =   8:42 p.m. – 30 hr. & 13 min. =

10:20 a.m. – 20 hr. & 57 min. =   8:40 a.m. – 41 hr. & 15 min. =

6:37 p.m. – 32 hr. & 21 min. =   9:18 p.m. – 26 hr. & 35 min. =

6:15 p.m. – 28 hr. & 19 min. =   8:46 a.m. – 29 hr. & 49 min. =

9:37 a.m. – 44 hr. & 36 min. =   4:26 a.m. – 12 hr. =

8:05 a.m. – 33 hr. & 54 min. =   4:38 p.m. – 38 hr. & 37 min. =

4:29 a.m. – 50 hr. & 24 min. =   6:28 a.m. – 35 hr. & 30 min. =

1:09 a.m. – 52 hr. & 47 min. =   10:04 a.m. – 29 hr. & 14 min. =

4:14 a.m. – 27 hr. & 18 min. =   9:36 a.m. – 50 hr. & 23 min. =

9:47 p.m. – 36 hr. & 58 min. =   3:41 p.m. – 42 hr. & 36 min. =

3:00 a.m. – 56 hr. & 31 min. =   9:48 a.m. – 27 hr. & 24 min. =

7:33 p.m. – 23 hr. & 9 min. =   8:48 a.m. – 45 hr. & 13 min. =

10:34 p.m. – 10 hr. & 55 min. =   12:12 a.m. – 40 hr. & 3 min. =

10:52 p.m. – 37 hr. & 52 min. =   7:21 a.m. – 44 hr. & 43 min. =

noon – 3 hr. & 48 min. =   10:49 p.m. – 19 hr. & 17 min. =

Chapter 5: Practice Finding the Number of Hours and Minutes between Times

Notes: This chapter is different. Now you are given two times and trying to figure out by how many hours and minutes they differ. Your answer will be in hours and minutes, but will not be expressed in clock format. Note that the order of the times is important.

Instructions:
- First subtract the minutes following the strategy from Chapter 2. Remember that you must subtract one hour when you borrow 60 minutes.
- Next subtract the hours.
- If one time is p.m. and the other is a.m., you need to trade one for 12 hours.
- If you need to borrow hours, you add 24 hours if both times are a.m. or if both times are p.m., but add 12 hours if one time was a.m. and the other was p.m.
- If your answer has 24 or more hours, subtract 24 hours from your answer.

Example 1: Subtract 4:32 a.m. from 9:57 a.m.
　　First we subtract the minutes: $57 - 32 = 25$ min. Next we subtract the hours: $9 - 4 = 5$ hr. The answer is 5 hr. & 25 min.

Example 2: Subtract 5:30 p.m. from 7:15 p.m.
　　15 minutes are not enough to subtract 30 minutes. We borrow 60 minutes, increasing the minutes to $15 + 60 = 75$ min. and reducing the hours to $7 - 1 = 6$ hr. Now we subtract the minutes: $75 - 30 = 45$ min. Next we subtract the hours: $6 - 5 = 1$ hr. The answer is 1 hr. & 45 min.

Example 3: Subtract 11:11 a.m. from 3:14 a.m.
　　First we subtract the minutes: $14 - 11 = 3$ min. 3 hours are not enough to subtract 11 hours. We borrow 24 hours since both times are a.m., increasing the hours to $3 + 24 = 27$ hr. Now we subtract the hours: $27 - 11 = 16$ hr. The answer is 16 hr. & 3 min.

Example 4: Subtract 9:55 p.m. from 2:20 a.m.
　　20 minutes are not enough to subtract 55 minutes. We borrow 60 minutes, increasing the minutes to $20 + 60 = 80$ min. and reducing the hours to $2 - 1 = 1$ hr. Now we subtract the minutes: $80 - 55 = 25$ min. 1 hour is not enough to subtract 9 hours. We borrow 12 hours since one time is a.m. and the other is p.m., increasing the hours to $1 + 12 = 13$ hr. Now we subtract the hours: $13 - 9 = 4$ hr. The answer is 4 hr. & 25 min.

4:19 a.m. – 8:58 a.m. =

1:30 p.m. – 10:07 a.m. =

11:08 p.m. – 7:12 a.m. =

1:57 p.m. – 3:45 a.m. =

6:29 a.m. – 9:26 p.m. =

11:11 a.m. – 10:49 p.m. =

3:11 a.m. – 6:00 p.m. =

6:55 p.m. – 12:03 p.m. =

9:39 a.m. – 11:31 a.m. =

2:57 a.m. – 6:05 a.m. =

8:49 a.m. – 9:01 a.m. =   1:22 a.m. – 10:18 p.m. =

11:58 p.m. – 5:52 p.m. =   10:34 a.m. – 3:08 p.m. =

1:08 p.m. – 12:16 a.m. =   9:51 p.m. – 9:29 p.m. =

5:09 a.m. – 1:30 p.m. =   9:53 p.m. – 8:57 a.m. =

4:50 a.m. – 11:54 p.m. =   12:38 a.m. – 4:06 a.m. =

9:38 p.m. – 9:20 a.m. =   1:20 a.m. – 2:09 p.m. =

4:25 p.m. – 1:43 p.m. =   9:17 a.m. – 12:21 p.m. =

10:15 a.m. – 9:04 a.m. =   12:45 p.m. – 12:22 a.m. =

3:22 a.m. – 11:09 p.m. =   8:03 a.m. – 5:50 p.m. =

5:40 a.m. – 12:29 p.m. =   8:37 p.m. – 7:12 p.m. =

11:59 a.m. – 4:39 p.m. =   7:41 p.m. – 9:54 a.m. =

7:32 a.m. – 3:37 p.m. =   12:24 p.m. – 7:01 p.m. =

2:30 a.m. – 9:22 a.m. =   6:11 a.m. – 2:46 p.m. =

10:36 p.m. – 2:33 a.m. =   1:27 p.m. – 5:28 p.m. =

8:14 a.m. – 10:50 p.m. =   12:01 a.m. – 4:58 p.m. =

7:13 p.m. – 6:17 p.m. =   6:56 a.m. – 12:15 a.m. =

2:05 p.m. – 7:48 p.m. =   1:25 p.m. – 8:32 a.m. =

10:52 p.m. – 5:49 a.m. =   11:48 p.m. – 7:36 p.m. =

3:24 p.m. – 7:38 a.m. =   5:05 a.m. – 1:56 a.m. =

6:46 a.m. – 6:32 a.m. =   9:40 a.m. – 10:47 a.m. =

9:33 p.m. – 2:08 a.m. =   2:41 a.m. – 9:33 p.m. =

3:41 p.m. – 11:25 p.m. =   7:24 p.m. – 12:28 p.m. =

4:45 a.m. – 1:02 p.m. =   10:27 a.m. – 8:17 p.m. =

5:37 p.m. – 8:42 a.m. =   8:40 p.m. – 11:42 a.m. =

1:21 p.m. – 4:07 a.m. =   12:59 a.m. – 6:08 p.m. =

10:04 a.m. – 5:53 a.m. =

7:47 p.m. – 6:33 p.m. =

9:33 a.m. – 1:18 a.m. =

3:02 p.m. – 3:05 a.m. =

9:10 a.m. – 2:33 p.m. =

9:22 a.m. – 4:05 a.m. =

6:49 a.m. – 4:10 p.m. =

1:28 a.m. – 1:50 p.m. =

6:05 a.m. – 8:53 a.m. =

12:05 p.m. – 7:15 p.m. =

1:50 p.m. – 1:08 p.m. =

5:05 p.m. – 4:29 p.m. =

8:05 p.m. – 2:25 p.m. =

4:15 p.m. – 11:20 p.m. =

8:40 p.m. – 10:17 a.m. =

2:46 p.m. – 7:26 a.m. =

9:17 p.m. – 4:08 p.m. =

3:33 p.m. – 11:21 a.m. =

2:05 p.m. – 11:21 a.m. =

4:18 a.m. – 9:06 p.m. =

7:42 p.m. – 7:18 a.m. =   2:30 a.m. – 4:17 p.m. =

3:27 a.m. – 10:50 p.m. =   4:29 a.m. – 5:48 a.m. =

2:56 p.m. – 10:50 a.m. =   3:16 p.m. – 5:03 p.m. =

2:19 p.m. – 6:21 a.m. =   2:20 a.m. – 4:59 a.m. =

9:31 a.m. – 6:15 p.m. =   6:09 a.m. – 8:33 p.m. =

2:44 p.m. – 7:01 a.m. =   6:17 p.m. – 2:16 a.m. =

3:36 a.m. – 4:20 a.m. =   7:28 a.m. – 2:54 a.m. =

4:37 a.m. – 11:06 p.m. =   1:07 a.m. – 4:09 p.m. =

5:20 a.m. – 4:46 p.m. =   3:52 a.m. – 10:20 p.m. =

2:57 a.m. – 7:01 a.m. =   7:07 a.m. – 11:06 a.m. =

3:54 a.m. – 9:12 a.m. =   10:28 a.m. – 1:55 p.m. =

6:57 a.m. – 8:19 a.m. =   1:18 p.m. – 1:48 p.m. =

10:53 a.m. – 12:50 a.m. =   7:57 p.m. – 2:09 p.m. =

11:32 a.m. – 11:20 p.m. =   12:01 p.m. – 4:27 a.m. =

1:02 p.m. – 12:31 a.m. =   2:22 a.m. – 2:11 a.m. =

11:26 p.m. – 12:50 p.m. =   8:39 p.m. – 2:08 a.m. =

10:49 p.m. – 5:08 a.m. =   4:39 a.m. – 8:10 p.m. =

10:31 p.m. – 6:28 p.m. =   10:22 a.m. – 11:01 p.m. =

8:48 p.m. – 12:16 p.m. =   8:26 p.m. – 12:05 p.m. =

7:51 a.m. – 1:17 a.m. =   6:40 p.m. – 10:32 a.m. =

1:58 p.m. – 2:24 a.m. =

4:57 p.m. – 6:26 a.m. =

10:42 a.m. – 2:56 a.m. =

4:15 p.m. – 11:17 a.m. =

1:12 a.m. – 8:37 p.m. =

4:25 a.m. – 11:13 p.m. =

4:11 a.m. – 12:09 a.m. =

10:54 a.m. – 11:38 p.m. =

6:40 p.m. – 3:21 p.m. =

10:39 a.m. – 1:58 p.m. =

2:06 p.m. – 10:59 a.m. =   4:02 p.m. – 8:32 p.m. =

11:28 p.m. – 9:04 a.m. =   5:01 p.m. – 2:08 p.m. =

9:30 p.m. – 9:49 a.m. =   12:06 a.m. – 8:15 p.m. =

6:50 a.m. – 8:16 p.m. =   8:57 p.m. – 11:48 p.m. =

10:47 p.m. – 2:03 p.m. =   3:05 p.m. – 2:10 a.m. =

9:43 a.m. – 12:06 p.m. =

6:03 p.m. – 1:38 a.m. =

5:32 p.m. – 6:27 a.m. =

4:56 p.m. – 7:52 a.m. =

10:34 p.m. – 3:44 a.m. =

11:32 p.m. – 6:33 a.m. =

6:40 a.m. – 11:49 a.m. =

6:23 p.m. – 6:58 p.m. =

10:00 a.m. – 6:03 p.m. =

10:21 a.m. – 1:42 a.m. =

2:04 p.m. − 8:03 p.m. =

11:38 a.m. − 2:58 p.m. =

10:21 a.m. − 11:22 p.m. =

3:13 a.m. − 4:10 p.m. =

4:34 p.m. − 11:15 a.m. =

4:06 a.m. − 8:57 p.m. =

11:27 p.m. − 12:54 p.m. =

8:42 p.m. − 6:33 p.m. =

6:44 a.m. − 1:41 p.m. =

12:17 a.m. − 5:12 p.m. =

11:52 a.m. – 5:49 p.m. =   11:03 a.m. – 10:08 a.m. =

10:56 p.m. – 9:37 a.m. =   12:15 a.m. – 10:23 p.m. =

3:33 p.m. – 1:41 a.m. =   4:41 p.m. – 3:23 p.m. =

12:13 a.m. – 10:40 a.m. =   12:57 a.m. – 12:14 p.m. =

6:19 p.m. – 12:07 p.m. =   8:58 a.m. – 12:46 a.m. =

11:38 p.m. – 12:56 a.m. =   3:11 p.m. – 1:36 p.m. =

4:17 p.m. – 8:05 p.m. =   7:11 p.m. – 3:59 p.m. =

6:41 p.m. – 5:41 a.m. =   9:36 p.m. – 5:31 a.m. =

5:29 a.m. – 11:13 a.m. =   8:35 p.m. – 1:19 a.m. =

8:11 a.m. – 11:04 a.m. =   12:38 p.m. – 8:19 p.m. =

6:52 a.m. – 10:12 a.m. =   10:13 a.m. – 8:05 p.m. =

6:38 a.m. – 4:30 a.m. =   9:22 p.m. – 11:26 p.m. =

3:22 p.m. – 8:52 a.m. =   1:01 p.m. – 3:20 a.m. =

12:12 p.m. – 11:42 a.m. =   7:06 p.m. – 9:23 p.m. =

7:00 p.m. – 10:06 a.m. =   9:40 p.m. – 8:15 a.m. =

5:49 p.m. – 8:25 a.m. =   5:50 p.m. – 8:48 p.m. =

9:03 a.m. – 12:09 p.m. =   12:15 a.m. – 12:52 a.m. =

7:49 p.m. – 3:20 a.m. =   4:07 a.m. – 6:39 a.m. =

10:45 p.m. – 2:15 p.m. =   7:15 a.m. – 1:39 p.m. =

12:16 a.m. – 12:12 a.m. =   1:03 a.m. – 3:59 p.m. =

3:33 a.m. – 1:01 p.m. =   8:54 p.m. – 3:43 a.m. =

12:11 a.m. – 7:14 a.m. =   6:51 p.m. – 8:24 a.m. =

8:52 a.m. – 5:26 a.m. =   10:30 a.m. – 2:15 p.m. =

2:09 a.m. – 1:01 a.m. =   7:34 p.m. – 9:41 a.m. =

4:14 p.m. – 12:18 p.m. =   5:46 a.m. – 6:53 p.m. =

3:15 p.m. – 1:14 p.m. =   8:49 p.m. – 8:22 p.m. =

2:08 p.m. – 4:38 a.m. =   5:48 a.m. – 2:21 a.m. =

10:00 p.m. – 8:41 p.m. =   11:44 a.m. – 4:06 a.m. =

9:23 p.m. – 6:58 p.m. =   4:56 p.m. – 6:54 p.m. =

11:58 p.m. – 11:28 p.m. =   10:36 p.m. – 5:32 p.m. =

5:26 p.m. – 12:25 p.m. =   10:28 p.m. – 12:32 p.m. =

11:40 p.m. – 7:09 p.m. =   1:43 a.m. – 2:49 p.m. =

9:47 p.m. – 2:21 a.m. =   9:41 a.m. – 1:58 p.m. =

5:56 p.m. – 8:59 a.m. =   4:37 a.m. – 9:46 a.m. =

11:43 a.m. – 4:33 p.m. =   10:43 a.m. – 2:52 p.m. =

3:21 p.m. – 5:06 a.m. =   8:44 a.m. – 11:55 p.m. =

9:24 p.m. – 5:04 a.m. =   11:39 a.m. – 4:00 a.m. =

11:19 a.m. – 3:39 a.m. =   1:10 p.m. – 11:01 p.m. =

5:25 p.m. – 4:53 p.m. =   10:25 a.m. – 9:38 p.m. =

3:41 a.m. – 5:00 a.m. =   8:14 p.m. – 5:56 a.m. =

12:53 p.m. – 10:24 a.m. =   12:59 p.m. – 11:13 p.m. =

9:42 p.m. – 1:50 p.m. =   1:53 a.m. – 8:15 a.m. =

3:32 p.m. – 8:43 p.m. =   2:50 a.m. – 4:08 p.m. =

3:07 p.m. – 5:16 p.m. =   9:05 p.m. – 7:47 p.m. =

9:27 p.m. – 5:15 p.m. =   6:34 a.m. – 3:09 p.m. =

Answer Key

Chapter 1 Answers:

Page 6
> 9:36 a.m., 1:29 p.m.
> 8:40 p.m., 1:00 a.m.
> 1:22 a.m., 3:01 a.m.
> 11:38 p.m., noon
> 1:44 a.m., 6:49 p.m.

Page 7
> 3:05 a.m., 8:17 p.m.
> 12:05 a.m., 2:17 a.m.
> 3:23 p.m., 8:50 a.m.
> 5:09 p.m., 5:38 p.m.
> 9:38 a.m., 11:59 p.m.

Page 8
> 11:00 p.m., 7:11 p.m.
> 8:26 p.m., 1:54 a.m.
> 11:45 p.m., 11:03 a.m.
> 11:55 p.m., 3:22 p.m.
> 8:24 p.m., 1:09 p.m.

Page 9
> 9:08 a.m., 10:19 p.m.
> 8:55 p.m., 5:00 a.m.
> 9:47 a.m., 6:42 p.m.
> 4:35 a.m., 1:04 p.m.
> 1:33 a.m., 1:48 p.m.

Page 10
> 5:20 a.m., 12:21 a.m.
> 9:31 a.m., 6:32 a.m.
> 2:34 a.m., 7:20 a.m.
> 10:32 p.m., 10:28 p.m.
> 2:32 p.m., 12:12 a.m.

Page 11
> 8:16 a.m., 6:07 p.m.
> 7:49 a.m., 4:56 a.m.
> 6:33 a.m., 4:00 a.m.
> 5:03 a.m., 10:12 p.m.
> 3:16 p.m., 8:48 p.m.

Page 12
> 7:23 p.m., 11:18 a.m.
> 4:10 a.m., 7:16 p.m.
> 3:00 a.m., 2:05 a.m.
> 7:30 a.m., 3:51 p.m.
> 6:39 p.m., 5:21 p.m.

Page 13
> 8:56 p.m., 1:15 a.m.
> 1:56 p.m., 7:11 p.m.
> 12:50 a.m., 6:58 p.m.
> 9:52 p.m., 5:17 a.m.
> 5:08 p.m., 2:46 p.m.

Page 14
> 7:20 p.m., 5:18 p.m.
> 10:09 p.m., 9:43 p.m.
> 9:52 a.m., 1:15 p.m.
> 9:48 a.m., 1:01 a.m.
> 7:08 a.m., 6:38 p.m.

Page 15
> 5:58 a.m., 12:23 p.m.
> 11:43 p.m., 3:59 p.m.
> 3:38 p.m., 2:25 a.m.
> 3:31 a.m., 8:53 a.m.
> 1:46 a.m., 8:59 p.m.

Page 16
> 4:00 a.m., 7:37 a.m.
> 11:46 a.m., 12:55 p.m.
> 8:23 a.m., 9:02 p.m.
> 12:38 p.m., 3:14 a.m.
> 10:11 a.m., 11:26 p.m.

Page 17
> 1:04 a.m., 11:10 p.m.
> 7:38 a.m., 4:18 p.m.
> 4:52 p.m., 7:51 p.m.
> 10:35 a.m., 11:33 a.m.
> 10:30 p.m., 3:16 p.m.

Page 18
> 4:25 p.m., 11:11 a.m.
> 1:14 a.m., 9:54 p.m.
> 1:29 p.m., 11:29 a.m.
> 5:23 a.m., 6:49 a.m.
> 10:54 p.m., 11:45 p.m.

Page 19
> 11:20 p.m., 12:22 p.m.
> 9:32 a.m., 1:24 a.m.
> 4:46 a.m., 5:34 p.m.
> 1:00 a.m., 6:18 p.m.
> 4:16 p.m., 6:26 p.m.

Page 20
> 10:40 p.m., 8:01 a.m.
> 7:41 a.m., 2:25 a.m.
> 12:21 a.m., 1:44 a.m.
> 6:40 p.m., 9:14 p.m.
> 1:26 a.m., 8:16 a.m.

Page 21
> 12:46 p.m., 9:28 a.m.
> 2:19 a.m., 6:25 p.m.
> 3:08 a.m., 2:55 p.m.
> 6:10 p.m., 2:01 p.m.
> 2:30 a.m., 8:14 a.m.

Page 22
> 2:48 p.m., 8:14 a.m.
> 8:54 p.m., 8:42 p.m.
> 1:39 a.m., 1:25 p.m.
> 9:30 a.m., 4:55 p.m.
> 5:07 p.m., 1:24 a.m.

Page 23

3:59 p.m., 9:26 p.m.
7:50 a.m., 10:11 p.m.
10:35 a.m., 11:14 p.m.
11:59 p.m., 6:33 a.m.
7:36 p.m., 9:47 p.m.

Page 24

6:55 p.m., 9:21 a.m.
8:24 a.m., 11:44 a.m.
9:19 p.m., 1:16 a.m.
1:06 p.m., 3:43 p.m.
1:21 a.m., 10:46 p.m.

Page 25

7:04 p.m., 12:47 a.m.
5:07 a.m., 2:37 p.m.
6:32 p.m., 6:49 a.m.
8:43 a.m., 2:45 p.m.
10:41 p.m., 6:37 a.m.

Page 26

12:14 a.m., 9:29 p.m.
6:11 p.m., 9:54 a.m.
8:12 a.m., 12:50 a.m.
12:29 p.m., 7:08 p.m.
9:27 a.m., 11:26 a.m.

Page 27

11:31 a.m., 10:40 a.m.
4:11 a.m., 1:31 p.m.
11:52 a.m., 5:24 a.m.
5:46 a.m., 8:46 p.m.
6:44 a.m., 3:24 p.m.

Page 28

7:13 a.m., 9:02 p.m.
5:44 p.m., 9:55 p.m.
9:26 a.m., 1:14 p.m.
3:05 a.m., 8:31 p.m.
5:31 p.m., 5:02 p.m.

Page 29

11:17 p.m., 12:49 p.m.
11:39 p.m., 1:37 a.m.
12:22 a.m., 10:26 a.m.
12:26 p.m., 3:19 p.m.
12:26 p.m., 8:08 p.m.

Page 30

3:51 a.m., 7:30 p.m.
2:35 a.m., 3:06 a.m.
10:35 p.m., 4:17 p.m.
11:50 a.m., 10:45 p.m.
7:54 a.m., 9:39 a.m.

Chapter 2 Answers:

Page 32

3:53 a.m., 12:28 p.m.
6:46 a.m., 1:46 a.m.
5:40 a.m., 1:28 p.m.
10:38 p.m., 7:56 a.m.
8:57 a.m., 10:06 p.m.

Page 33

11:18 p.m., 11:38 p.m.
3:12 a.m., 2:37 a.m.
12:03 p.m., 2:48 a.m.
3:46 p.m., 1:52 p.m.
9:37 a.m., 5:50 a.m.

Page 34

4:42 p.m., 3:39 p.m.
3:47 a.m., 10:09 p.m.
6:54 a.m., 9:23 p.m.
7:48 a.m., 6:48 a.m.
3:18 p.m., 12:41 a.m.

Page 35

5:18 a.m., 4:17 p.m.
12:29 p.m., 6:26 a.m.
2:15 a.m., 12:19 a.m.
1:36 a.m., 1:50 a.m.
2:00 p.m., 4:17 p.m.

Page 36

3:18 p.m., 3:34 a.m.
4:48 p.m., 10:38 p.m.
2:53 a.m., 4:41 p.m.
12:32 a.m., 8:32 p.m.
7:20 a.m., 12:24 p.m.

Page 37

12:55 p.m., 8:58 p.m.
12:54 a.m., 4:02 p.m.
6:37 a.m., 8:38 a.m.
2:59 a.m., 6:00 p.m.
10:56 p.m., 3:20 a.m.

Page 38

3:56 a.m., 7:21 p.m.
10:51 a.m., 3:01 p.m.
9:08 a.m., 11:52 p.m.
8:41 p.m., 7:01 p.m.
2:34 a.m., 3:54 a.m.

Page 39

1:15 p.m., 2:17 p.m.
12:16 a.m., 8:37 p.m.
12:43 p.m., 7:33 p.m.
4:17 p.m., 4:47 a.m.
3:36 p.m., 1:48 p.m.

Page 40

6:04 p.m., 4:47 a.m.
7:57 p.m., 8:28 p.m.
4:04 a.m., 6:16 a.m.
5:28 p.m., 4:43 p.m.
10:03 a.m., 5:00 a.m.

Page 41

6:16 a.m., 7:57 p.m.
6:04 a.m., 8:26 p.m.
1:19 a.m., 10:30 p.m.
4:00 p.m., 8:12 a.m.
8:46 p.m., 8:13 a.m.

Page 42

8:12 a.m., 5:21 a.m.
11:35 a.m., 4:23 a.m.
11:04 a.m., 11:21 a.m.
5:32 a.m., 5:36 p.m.
10:49 p.m., 6:39 p.m.

Page 43

10:56 a.m., 1:46 a.m.
10:30 a.m., 3:52 a.m.
10:25 a.m., 8:33 p.m.
3:41 p.m., 8:30 p.m.
9:49 a.m., 4:30 p.m.

Page 44

12:44 p.m., 12:17 a.m.
5:45 p.m., 6:01 p.m.
6:54 p.m., 4:28 p.m.
1:23 p.m., 6:20 a.m.
10:24 p.m., 6:50 a.m.

Page 45

12:34 a.m., 10:19 p.m.
4:18 a.m., 11:06 p.m.
11:51 p.m., 1:19 a.m.
6:58 a.m., 3:51 p.m.
6:10 p.m., 1:18 p.m.

Page 46

11:33 p.m., 2:39 p.m.
9:59 p.m., 1:11 p.m.
4:09 p.m., 6:34 a.m.
6:45 p.m., 3:11 p.m.
7:32 p.m., 7:55 a.m.

Page 47

1:14 p.m., 3:25 a.m.
4:02 a.m., 4:27 a.m.
5:35 p.m., 12:41 p.m.
12:11 a.m., 1:33 p.m.
8:06 p.m., 9:24 p.m.

Page 48

2:40 a.m., 5:22 p.m.
5:37 p.m., 8:10 p.m.
6:49 p.m., 1:36 a.m.
4:37 a.m., 11:09 p.m.
7:00 a.m., 12:58 p.m.

Page 49

10:44 p.m., 8:57 a.m.
6:28 p.m., 10:59 a.m.
5:21 a.m., 10:45 a.m.
12:35 a.m., 5:25 a.m.
2:43 p.m., 7:43 p.m.

Page 50

1:53 a.m., 12:31 a.m.
6:25 p.m., 6:03 a.m.
8:14 p.m., 12:02 a.m.
1:55 a.m., 8:28 a.m.
1:13 p.m., 11:10 a.m.

Page 51

1:39 a.m., 8:52 a.m.
2:35 p.m., 10:11 a.m.
3:41 a.m., 2:37 p.m.
11:38 a.m., 4:15 a.m.
11:57 a.m., 11:44 p.m.

Page 52

8:08 p.m., 8:19 a.m.
6:22 p.m., 3:26 p.m.
4:04 a.m., 7:57 p.m.
2:18 p.m., 8:23 a.m.
11:55 a.m., 12:03 a.m.

Page 53

4:24 a.m., 1:17 a.m.
7:20 a.m., 8:06 a.m.
2:24 a.m., 5:13 p.m.
11:03 p.m., 2:03 p.m.
3:31 a.m., 9:39 a.m.

Page 54

9:57 a.m., 5:27 p.m.
9:10 a.m., 9:55 p.m.
11:57 a.m., 6:58 p.m.
2:45 a.m., 6:00 a.m.
9:10 p.m., 8:51 a.m.

Page 55

9:09 a.m., 8:33 a.m.
11:14 a.m., 8:04 p.m.
5:35 a.m., 11:56 p.m.
7:02 a.m., 6:46 a.m.
3:23 a.m., 8:58 a.m.

Page 56

3:15 a.m., 4:23 a.m.
12:46 a.m., 8:48 p.m.
11:07 p.m., 9:57 p.m.
2:56 a.m., 4:44 p.m.
1:01 p.m., 11:29 a.m.

Chapter 3 Answers:

Page 58

6:25 a.m., 5:43 a.m.
1:44 a.m., 12:15 p.m.
5:06 a.m., 2:23 p.m.
1:47 p.m., 11:11 a.m.
2:40 a.m., 3:14 p.m.

Page 59

1:49 p.m., 2:40 a.m.
1:33 a.m., 8:38 p.m.
1:56 a.m., 7:31 a.m.
2:44 a.m., 9:12 p.m.
10:32 a.m., 10:15 a.m.

Page 60

1:37 a.m., 7:05 p.m.
11:53 p.m., 10:55 p.m.
7:13 p.m., 7:09 p.m.
1:07 p.m., 1:45 p.m.
11:38 p.m., 5:23 a.m.

Page 61
>   4:37 p.m., 3:44 a.m.
>   6:01 a.m., 9:44 p.m.
>   12:28 p.m., 3:41 a.m.
>   6:38 p.m., 5:08 a.m.
>   6:51 p.m., 7:29 p.m.

Page 62
>   12:33 p.m., 2:27 a.m.
>   9:43 a.m., 9:39 a.m.
>   2:07 p.m., 2:09 p.m.
>   7:04 p.m., 11:54 p.m.
>   10:46 p.m., 4:44 p.m.

Page 63
>   11:29 a.m., 7:24 a.m.
>   2:54 a.m., 7:01 p.m.
>   5:49 a.m., 1:51 a.m.
>   10:46 p.m., 12:51 a.m.
>   1:27 a.m., 11:05 a.m.

Page 64
>   10:20 p.m., 10:04 a.m.
>   12:09 p.m., 9:39 a.m.
>   8:15 p.m., 8:00 p.m.
>   7:35 a.m., 7:27 p.m.
>   3:33 a.m., 4:30 p.m.

Page 65
>   1:29 p.m., 5:47 a.m.
>   12:15 a.m., 6:06 a.m.
>   5:41 a.m., 4:36 p.m.
>   4:17 a.m., 8:30 p.m.
>   9:48 p.m., 4:13 p.m.

Page 66
>   10:07 p.m., 11:26 p.m.
>   8:56 p.m., 2:10 p.m.
>   3:25 a.m., 9:04 p.m.
>   10:33 p.m., 1:31 a.m.
>   8:43 p.m., 7:33 a.m.

Page 67
>   7:10 p.m., 8:18 p.m.
>   10:30 p.m., 3:52 a.m.
>   6:38 a.m., 2:34 a.m.
>   12:55 p.m., 7:33 p.m.
>   5:13 p.m., 4:25 p.m.

Page 68
>   10:24 a.m., 12:44 p.m.
>   6:54 a.m., 11:51 p.m.
>   11:00 a.m., 4:54 a.m.
>   10:39 a.m., 4:14 a.m.
>   11:13 p.m., 11:05 p.m.

Page 69
>   10:56 a.m., 10:01 a.m.
>   7:14 a.m., 10:39 p.m.
>   12:46 a.m., 12:19 p.m.
>   7:49 a.m., 1:35 p.m.
>   1:40 p.m., 7:01 a.m.

Page 70
>   7:55 a.m., 4:42 p.m.
>   1:13 a.m., 5:22 a.m.
>   2:33 p.m., 11:39 p.m.
>   2:55 p.m., 6:33 p.m.
>   5:35 a.m., 7:06 p.m.

Page 71
>   2:18 a.m., 6:50 a.m.
>   12:29 p.m., 12:08 p.m.
>   5:35 a.m., 5:55 a.m.
>   7:35 a.m., 10:12 p.m.
>   7:01 a.m., 11:32 a.m.

Page 72
>   2:21 p.m., 8:40 p.m.
>   9:03 p.m., 12:47 a.m.
>   11:45 p.m., 5:39 p.m.
>   9:55 p.m., 8:39 p.m.
>   12:58 a.m., 10:17 p.m.

Page 73
>   8:37 a.m., 6:07 a.m.
>   8:39 a.m., 5:01 p.m.
>   5:13 p.m., 11:11 p.m.
>   5:39 p.m., 3:50 a.m.
>   2:14 a.m., 8:00 a.m.

Page 74
>   11:28 a.m., 9:46 p.m.
>   3:36 p.m., 8:05 p.m.
>   12:51 p.m., 1:25 p.m.
>   12:14 a.m., 2:26 a.m.
>   4:52 p.m., 2:46 a.m.

Page 75
>   1:43 p.m., 3:18 a.m.
>   11:39 a.m., 11:42 a.m.
>   7:25 p.m., 4:11 p.m.
>   2:04 a.m., 6:32 a.m.
>   8:16 p.m., 8:10 p.m.

Page 76
>   11:23 a.m., 10:03 p.m.
>   3:27 a.m., 12:08 p.m.
>   1:47 a.m., 5:27 p.m.
>   2:28 a.m., 7:51 p.m.
>   9:52 a.m., 9:24 p.m.

Page 77
>   2:13 p.m., 5:15 p.m.
>   10:47 p.m., 3:53 a.m.
>   12:16 a.m., 11:15 a.m.
>   9:49 p.m., 5:20 a.m.
>   5:08 p.m., 11:43 a.m.

Page 78
>   6:17 a.m., 6:45 p.m.
>   4:29 a.m., 9:02 p.m.
>   6:49 p.m., 7:56 a.m.
>   4:12 p.m., 4:21 p.m.
>   11:47 p.m., 3:56 p.m.

Page 79
    4:09 p.m., 8:58 p.m.
    5:40 a.m., 5:42 a.m.
    12:03 p.m., 2:58 a.m.
    6:56 p.m., 8:33 a.m.
    5:33 a.m., 9:37 a.m.

Page 80
    12:28 a.m., 4:14 a.m.
    1:25 p.m., 9:44 p.m.
    4:29 a.m., 10:15 p.m.
    1:06 p.m., 2:13 p.m.
    8:35 a.m., 7:30 p.m.

Page 81
    11:02 a.m., 11:32 p.m.
    4:19 p.m., 3:04 a.m.
    11:33 a.m., 1:33 p.m.
    9:42 a.m., 5:03 p.m.
    9:08 a.m., 9:21 a.m.

Page 82
    8:20 a.m., 12:12 p.m.
    1:14 a.m., 5:12 a.m.
    6:54 p.m., 11:39 a.m.
    10:31 p.m., 9:20 a.m.
    2:48 a.m., 8:16 p.m.

Chapter 4 Answers:

Page 84
    12:13 a.m., 8:23 a.m.
    4:53 a.m., 9:01 p.m.
    12:01 a.m., 2:22 a.m.
    1:26 a.m., 1:25 p.m.
    8:00 a.m., 10:25 a.m.

Page 85
    11:28 a.m., 3:30 p.m.
    3:47 a.m., 4:38 a.m.
    2:27 a.m., 6:45 a.m.
    12:57 a.m., 6:46 p.m.
    7:19 a.m., 8:16 p.m.

Page 86
    4:28 a.m., 8:10 a.m.
    9:58 a.m., 7:44 a.m.
    12:39 p.m., 7:49 a.m.
    3:42 a.m., 7:53 a.m.
    11:45 a.m., 12:15 p.m.

Page 87
    9:33 a.m., 4:08 a.m.
    10:36 a.m., 9:37 p.m.
    7:57 a.m., 8:56 p.m.
    2:46 p.m., 9:17 p.m.
    2:46 a.m., 10:16 p.m.

Page 88
    9:01 a.m., 6:16 a.m.
    8:58 p.m., 11:32 p.m.
    4:57 a.m., 11:07 a.m.
    5:45 a.m., 11:20 a.m.
    6:12 p.m., 9:59 p.m.

Page 89
    7:15 a.m., 12:59 p.m.
    12:34 p.m., 1:09 a.m.
    3:19 p.m., 4:25 p.m.
    11:06 p.m., 8:43 p.m.
    10:49 p.m., 4:11 p.m.

Page 90
    11:37 p.m., 2:07 a.m.
    9:35 a.m., 1:11 a.m.
    11:43 p.m., 11:53 p.m.
    2:10 a.m., 5:34 p.m.
    3:55 p.m., 2:00 a.m.

Page 91
    10:26 a.m., 3:04 p.m.
    12:40 p.m., 2:28 a.m.
    8:56 p.m., 7:44 p.m.
    8:14 a.m., 11:42 a.m.
    4:33 a.m., 9:33 p.m.

Page 92
    3:45 p.m., 9:54 p.m.
    5:13 a.m., 10:02 p.m.
    2:06 p.m., 11:19 p.m.
    5:27 a.m., 12:56 a.m.
    11:41 p.m., 3:13 a.m.

Page 93
    3:09 a.m., 12:20 a.m.
    3:34 p.m., 3:06 p.m.
    9:25 a.m., 7:45 a.m.
    3:39 p.m., 10:29 p.m.
    8:51 p.m., 12:40 a.m.

Page 94
    9:03 a.m., 10:44 a.m.
    9:16 p.m., 12:32 p.m.
    5:44 a.m., 2:53 p.m.
    10:13 p.m., 8:03 a.m.
    3:30 a.m., 2:25 a.m.

Page 95
    2:33 p.m., 9:25 p.m.
    3:59 a.m., 8:46 p.m.
    3:44 a.m., 10:26 p.m.
    9:50 p.m., 9:33 a.m.
    12:48 p.m., 7:16 a.m.

Page 96
    12:17 a.m., 2:49 a.m.
    11:17 a.m., 7:17 a.m.
    2:29 a.m., 3:19 p.m.
    12:56 p.m., 5:36 a.m.
    8:14 p.m., 6:26 a.m.

Page 97
    4:46 a.m., 3:08 a.m.
    3:11 a.m., 4:04 p.m.
    4:59 p.m., 9:27 p.m.
    2:04 a.m., 6:24 a.m.
    7:39 p.m., 4:15 p.m.

Page 98
9:10 p.m., 4:28 p.m.
5:40 p.m., 8:18 p.m.
5:38 p.m., 12:42 a.m.
12:21 a.m., 4:51 a.m.
10:26 a.m., 12:51 p.m.

Page 99
6:38 a.m., 12:37 a.m.
5:20 a.m., 7:58 a.m.
6:51 p.m., 4:41 p.m.
7:35 a.m., 11:29 a.m.
11:16 a.m., 6:03 p.m.

Page 100
4:09 p.m., 6:53 p.m.
7:01 p.m., 9:46 a.m.
1:20 p.m., 6:36 p.m.
8:21 a.m., 11:26 a.m.
2:51 p.m., 11:24 a.m.

Page 101
7:09 a.m., 11:16 p.m.
4:07 p.m., 4:32 p.m.
3:34 p.m., 7:18 p.m.
11:17 p.m., 1:00 a.m.
5:20 a.m., 8:44 a.m.

Page 102
6:26 a.m., 1:56 p.m.
9:54 a.m., 10:24 a.m.
6:20 p.m., 6:22 p.m.
10:57 a.m., 3:39 p.m.
1:05 p.m., 10:07 p.m.

Page 103
4:18 a.m., 1:50 p.m.
5:51 p.m., 10:51 a.m.
10:13 a.m., 5:44 p.m.
11:14 p.m., 1:42 p.m.
7:40 a.m., 9:10 a.m.

Page 104
6:59 p.m., 3:12 p.m.
7:30 p.m., 1:48 a.m.
8:08 p.m., 6:38 a.m.
noon, 12:20 p.m.
8:12 p.m., 3:18 p.m.

Page 105
7:24 p.m., 3:49 a.m.
2:22 a.m., 9:32 a.m.
10:39 a.m., 10:03 p.m.
10:52 a.m., 2:40 p.m.
4:42 p.m., 3:47 p.m.

Page 106
2:50 p.m., 2:29 p.m.
1:23 p.m., 3:25 p.m.
10:16 a.m., 6:43 p.m.
1:56 p.m., 2:57 a.m.
1:01 p.m., 4:26 p.m.

Page 107
10:11 p.m., 2:01 a.m.
2:05 a.m., 6:58 p.m.
8:22 p.m., 4:50 a.m.
12:56 a.m., 7:13 a.m.
8:49 a.m., 9:05 p.m.

Page 108
6:29 p.m., 6:24 a.m.
8:24 p.m., 11:35 a.m.
11:39 a.m., 8:09 a.m.
9:00 a.m., 10:38 a.m.
8:12 a.m., 3:32 a.m.

Chapter 5 Answers:

Page 110

    19 hr. & 21 min., 3 hr. & 23 min.

    15 hr. & 56 min., 10 hr. & 12 min.

    9 hr. & 3 min., 12 hr. & 22 min.

    9 hr. & 11 min., 6 hr. & 52 min.

    22 hr. & 8 min., 20 hr. & 52 min.

Page 111

    23 hr. & 48 min., 3 hr. & 4 min.

    6 hr. & 6 min., 19 hr. & 26 min.

    12 hr. & 52 min., 0 hr. & 22 min.

    15 hr. & 39 min., 12 hr. & 56 min.

    4 hr. & 56 min., 20 hr. & 32 min.

Page 112

    12 hr. & 18 min., 11 hr. & 11 min.

    2 hr. & 42 min., 20 hr. & 56 min.

    1 hr. & 11 min., 12 hr. & 23 min.

    4 hr. & 13 min., 14 hr. & 13 min.

    17 hr. & 11 min., 1 hr. & 25 min.

Page 113

    19 hr. & 20 min., 9 hr. & 47 min.

    15 hr. & 55 min., 17 hr. & 23 min.

    17 hr. & 8 min., 15 hr. & 25 min.

    20 hr. & 3 min., 19 hr. & 59 min.

    9 hr. & 24 min., 7 hr. & 3 min.

Page 114

    0 hr. & 56 min., 6 hr. & 41 min.

    18 hr. & 17 min., 4 hr. & 53 min.

    17 hr. & 3 min., 4 hr. & 12 min.

    7 hr. & 46 min., 3 hr. & 9 min.

    0 hr. & 14 min., 22 hr. & 53 min.

Page 115

    19 hr. & 25 min., 5 hr. & 8 min.

    16 hr. & 16 min., 6 hr. & 56 min.

    15 hr. & 43 min., 14 hr. & 10 min.

    8 hr. & 55 min., 8 hr. & 58 min.

    9 hr. & 14 min., 6 hr. & 51 min.

Page 116

    4 hr. & 11 min., 1 hr. & 14 min.

    8 hr. & 15 min., 11 hr. & 57 min.

    18 hr. & 37 min., 5 hr. & 17 min.

    14 hr. & 39 min., 11 hr. & 38 min.

    21 hr. & 12 min., 16 hr. & 50 min.

Page 117

    0 hr. & 42 min., 0 hr. & 36 min.

    5 hr. & 40 min., 16 hr. & 55 min.

    10 hr. & 23 min., 7 hr. & 20 min.

    5 hr. & 9 min., 4 hr. & 12 min.

    2 hr. & 44 min., 7 hr. & 12 min.

Page 118

    12 hr. & 24 min., 10 hr. & 13 min.

    4 hr. & 37 min., 22 hr. & 41 min.

    4 hr. & 6 min., 22 hr. & 13 min.

    7 hr. & 58 min., 21 hr. & 21 min.

    15 hr. & 16 min., 9 hr. & 36 min.

Page 119

    7 hr. & 43 min., 16 hr. & 1 min.

    23 hr. & 16 min., 4 hr. & 34 min.

    5 hr. & 31 min., 8 hr. & 58 min.

    12 hr. & 34 min., 5 hr. & 32 min.

    19 hr. & 56 min., 20 hr. & 1 min.

Page 120

    18 hr. & 42 min., 20 hr. & 33 min.

    22 hr. & 38 min., 23 hr. & 30 min.

    10 hr. & 3 min., 5 hr. & 48 min.

    12 hr. & 12 min., 7 hr. & 34 min.

    12 hr. & 31 min., 0 hr. & 11 min.

Page 121

    10 hr. & 36 min., 18 hr. & 31 min.

    17 hr. & 41 min., 8 hr. & 29 min.

    4 hr. & 3 min., 11 hr. & 21 min.

    8 hr. & 32 min., 8 hr. & 21 min.

    6 hr. & 34 min., 8 hr. & 8 min.

Page 122
    11 hr. & 34 min., 10 hr. & 31 min.
    7 hr. & 46 min., 4 hr. & 58 min.
    4 hr. & 35 min., 5 hr. & 12 min.
    4 hr. & 2 min., 11 hr. & 16 min.
    3 hr. & 19 min., 20 hr. & 41 min.

Page 123
    3 hr. & 7 min., 19 hr. & 30 min.
    14 hr. & 24 min., 2 hr. & 53 min.
    11 hr. & 41 min., 3 hr. & 51 min.
    10 hr. & 34 min., 21 hr. & 9 min.
    8 hr. & 44 min., 12 hr. & 55 min.

Page 124
    21 hr. & 37 min., 16 hr. & 25 min.
    11 hr. & 5 min., 9 hr. & 4 min.
    18 hr. & 50 min., 16 hr. & 59 min.
    18 hr. & 51 min., 23 hr. & 25 min.
    15 hr. & 57 min., 8 hr. & 39 min.

Page 125
    18 hr. & 1 min., 20 hr. & 40 min.
    10 hr. & 59 min., 11 hr. & 3 min.
    5 hr. & 19 min., 7 hr. & 9 min.
    10 hr. & 33 min., 2 hr. & 9 min.
    17 hr. & 3 min., 7 hr. & 5 min.

Page 126
    18 hr. & 3 min., 0 hr. & 55 min.
    13 hr. & 19 min., 1 hr. & 52 min.
    13 hr. & 52 min., 1 hr. & 18 min.
    13 hr. & 33 min., 12 hr. & 43 min.
    6 hr. & 12 min., 8 hr. & 12 min.

Page 127
    22 hr. & 42 min., 1 hr. & 35 min.
    20 hr. & 12 min., 3 hr. & 12 min.
    13 hr. & 0 min., 16 hr. & 5 min.
    18 hr. & 16 min., 19 hr. & 16 min.
    21 hr. & 7 min., 16 hr. & 19 min.

Page 128
    20 hr. & 40 min., 14 hr. & 8 min.
    2 hr. & 8 min., 21 hr. & 56 min.
    6 hr. & 30 min., 9 hr. & 41 min.
    0 hr. & 30 min., 21 hr. & 43 min.
    8 hr. & 54 min., 13 hr. & 25 min.

Page 129
    9 hr. & 24 min., 21 hr. & 2 min.
    20 hr. & 54 min., 23 hr. & 23 min.
    16 hr. & 29 min., 21 hr. & 28 min.
    8 hr. & 30 min., 17 hr. & 36 min.
    0 hr. & 4 min., 9 hr. & 4 min.

Page 130
    14 hr. & 32 min., 17 hr. & 11 min.
    16 hr. & 57 min., 10 hr. & 27 min.
    3 hr. & 26 min., 20 hr. & 15 min.
    1 hr. & 8 min., 9 hr. & 53 min.
    3 hr. & 56 min., 10 hr. & 53 min.

Page 131
    2 hr. & 1 min., 0 hr. & 27 min.
    9 hr. & 30 min., 3 hr. & 27 min.
    1 hr. & 19 min., 7 hr. & 38 min.
    2 hr. & 25 min., 22 hr. & 2 min.
    0 hr. & 30 min., 5 hr. & 4 min.

Page 132
    5 hr. & 1 min., 9 hr. & 56 min.
    4 hr. & 31 min., 10 hr. & 54 min.
    19 hr. & 26 min., 19 hr. & 43 min.
    8 hr. & 57 min., 18 hr. & 51 min.
    19 hr. & 10 min., 19 hr. & 51 min.

Page 133
    10 hr. & 15 min., 8 hr. & 49 min.
    16 hr. & 20 min., 7 hr. & 39 min.
    7 hr. & 40 min., 14 hr. & 9 min.
    0 hr. & 32 min., 12 hr. & 47 min.
    22 hr. & 41 min., 14 hr. & 18 min.

Page 134

     2 hr. & 29 min., 13 hr. & 46 min.
     7 hr. & 52 min., 17 hr. & 38 min.
     18 hr. & 49 min., 10 hr. & 42 min.
     21 hr. & 51 min., 1 hr. & 18 min.
     4 hr. & 12 min., 15 hr. & 25 min.